# Lead Fearlessly, Love Hard

# Lead Fearlessly, Love Hard

## FINDING YOUR PURPOSE AND PUTTING IT TO WORK

Linda Cliatt-Wayman

**JB** JOSSEY-BASS™

A Wiley Brand

Published by Jossey-Bass
A Wiley Brand
One Montgomery Street, Suite 1000, San Francisco, CA 94104-4594—www.josseybass.com

Jossey-Bass books and products are available through most bookstores. To contact Jossey-Bass
directly call our Customer Care Department within the U.S. at 800-956-7739, outside the U.S.
at 317-572-3986, or fax 317-572-4002.

Wiley publishes in a variety of print and electronic formats and by print-on-demand. Some
material included with standard print versions of this book may not be included in e-books or in
print-on-demand. If this book refers to media such as a CD or DVD that is not included in the
version you purchased, you may download this material at http://booksupport.wiley.com. For
more information about Wiley products, visit www.wiley.com.

**Library of Congress Cataloging-in-Publication Data**

Names: Cliatt-Wayman, Linda, 1961- author.
Title: Lead fearlessly, love hard : finding your purpose and putting it to
    work / Linda Cliatt-Wayman.
Description: San Francisco, CA : Jossey-Bass, 2017. | Includes index.
Identifiers: LCCN 2017008796 (print) | LCCN 2017012558 (ebook) | ISBN
    9781119288534 (cloth) | ISBN 9781119288831 (epdf) | ISBN 9781119288817
    (epub)
Subjects: LCSH: Educational leadership—United States. | School management
    and organization—United States.
Classification: LCC LB2806 .C5225 2017 (print) | LCC LB2806 (ebook) | DDC
    371.2—dc23
LC record available at https://lccn.loc.gov/2017008796

Cover design: Wiley
Cover image: © Ready Set Productions

Printed in the United States of America

FIRST EDITION

*HB Printing*   10  9  8  7  6  5  4  3  2  1

In memory of Mona Cliatt, my mom

Thank you for providing Andrea, Denise, and me with

the foundational tools to LEAD:

Faith, Love, and Education

# Contents

# Acknowledgments

I want to take this moment to thank my publisher, Jossey-Bass, for providing me with the forum to tell my leadership story. A very special thank you to my editor—Kate Bradford, copyeditor —Kathleen Miller, and production editor—Haritha Dharmarajan, who had the task of getting this book ready for publication. Their patience and insight were extraordinary. Thank you to the organizers of the Pennsylvania Conference for Women and TED .com for giving me the first platform to tell my leadership story.

To all of my leadership team members over the years—thank you for your dedication and intense focus on the success of every child under your care. Success happened because of all of you: Michelle Garcon-McCoy, Vanessa Green King, Annetta Jackson, Syida Johnson, Evan Kramp, Kenesta Mack, Jameka McGraw-Byrd, Melissa Schafer, Jacqueline Palone, Anna Shurak, Susan Skraitz, Jennifer Speirs-Robinson, Mike Spangenberg, Sonia Szymanski, Orick Smith, and Terri Wiley.

Thank you to my school police officer, Kevin Dancy, and to Philadelphia police officer William Eib, for keeping my students and staff safe each day, and for providing an exemplary model of commitment to the welfare of children for law enforcement officials everywhere.

To my wonderful family, my husband, Dana, my two precious daughters, Paige and Sasha, and my two sisters, Andrea and Denise—thank you for your unconditional love and patience during this project. To all of my friends, without your listening ear this could never have been accomplished. To my best friend, Winona Hurst-Waldon—thank you for your love, friendship, and unwavering support for over 30 years.

To Principals past and present—thank you for your selfless service to your students and this nation. Because of your sacrifice, children get to live their dream. How special is that?

And last, but certainly most important, I would like to thank God and his son Jesus for the source of my strength and the purpose for my life.

Sincerely,
Principal Wayman

# Introduction

**"You go!"** The voice in my head was so loud, bold, and so unusually clear that I stopped in the middle of the hallway and responded to the voice with a grammatically incorrect question: **"Me go?"**

**"You go!"** the voice repeated. As I walked slowly to my office, calm but confused, I kept repeating the words I heard from the voice, "You go, you go, you go!" With every step it became clearer to me that the reason why I could not find a candidate for principal was because I was the candidate. I was the leader I was waiting and searching for.

"Persistently dangerous" was the label placed on the school I was chosen to lead. As of March 2015, the Pennsylvania Department of Education lists a school as persistently dangerous on its website "if it exceeds a certain number of dangerous incidents in the most recent school year and in one additional year of the two years prior to the most recent school year." A dangerous incident has been defined as either "a weapons possession incident resulting in arrest (guns, knives, or other weapons) or a violent incident resulting in arrest (homicide, kidnapping, robbery, sexual offenses, and assaults)."[*]

---

[*]"Pennsylvania Unsafe School Choice Option: Frequently Asked Questions," last modified March 2015, www.education.pa.gov/Documents/Teachers-Administrators/No%20Child%20Left%20Behind/Unsafe%20School%20Choice%20Option%20FAQs.pdf/.

Strawberry Mansion High School persistently dangerous! Was it really?

From 2010–2012, I was Assistant Superintendent for High Schools in Philadelphia, the leader of 52 principals and 61,000 children. I joined a central office team that was already well underway in finding ways to cut costs in the school district budget. Their attention was fixated on the schools that were underutilized. A company was hired to collect data on each existing school building. They were charged with recording the building capacity of each school and comparing it to the number of students who were actually attending the school, as part of a project called the "Facility Master Plan."

After the company revealed their findings to the superintendent it was decided that one high school would close, another would relocate, and the two would merge into a third school, forming a three-way high school merger. There was one major problem with this plan—the decision was decided solely on building usage and financial gain, not the facts of each school involved in the merger.

The three schools that were set to merge were located in North Philadelphia, one of the most violent sections of Philadelphia. This area was known for its rival gangs, high drug use, high crime rate, and a poverty level that is among the highest in the nation. Sure, the school selected to house the three-way merger had wonderful features. It was huge. It had five floors, newly renovated science labs, a brand-new culinary facility, and a beautiful, new library. The construction of the building was ideal for a state-of-the-art school, but there was one more very important fact about Strawberry Mansion High School: it had been on the nation's Persistently Dangerous Schools list for five consecutive years.

It was my job as Assistant Superintendent for High Schools to research, locate, and hire the principal for the first three-way high school merger in the history of Philadelphia Public Schools. The area where the school resided was well known for its violence, so finding a principal was not going to be easy. After a national search for principals there were zero applicants for the job. As time passed, I made the painful decision that I would have to move another school leader out of an existing school to lead Strawberry Mansion High School. After careful review of all 52 principals, one candidate emerged. I called her in for a meeting to let her know that I had to move her out of her school and send her to Strawberry Mansion. She glared at me with grave concern and lifted up her shirt to display a small device on her hip—a heart monitor. "Mrs. Wayman," she said, "if I have to do it I will, but it may kill me." Without hesitation, my search for a principal resumed.

I started to believe that I would never find a principal to lead Strawberry Mansion High School. Then, I heard the voice say, "You go!" I walked back to my office and prepared to leave the central office for good. There was just one thing I had to do first. I had to inform the principals that I was departing. I gathered the principals for our last meeting of the year. I told them that I was honored to work with them and for them, but that I was leaving the post of assistant superintendent to return to the ranks as principal. The rumor had already circulated. I was just making it official. Then I announced that I would be the new Principal of Strawberry Mansion High School to oversee the merger of the three high schools in our division. I told them that the students in those three schools were my responsibility.

I was raised in North Philadelphia, blocks away from Strawberry Mansion High School, in poverty with my mom and two sisters. My mom always told us that education would be our only way out. She would often tell us "education can change your life." She was right. It changed my life. I experienced firsthand the transformational power of education and desperately wanted all of the 61,000 high school students in the School District of Philadelphia to experience that same power. My story from poverty to endless possibilities has helped form the purpose for my work, why I do what I do. It is my life purpose to pull as many children out of poverty as I can, even if the school they will attend is labeled "persistently dangerous."

Why do you do what you do? Why do you lead? What is the purpose in your leadership? These are some of the questions I want to address in this book.

I am also writing this book because there is so much focus on highlighting and decrying the myriad challenges facing educators today who choose to educate adolescents who live in poverty, yet there is very little information that focuses on how to succeed in spite of those daunting challenges. What has to be remembered is that there are literally millions of children whose lives depend on schools with all types of discouraging labels, so we have a moral imperative to succeed for them today, even in the midst of an incredibly imperfect system. So much of the heated debate about education is about improving systems from without. This book is intended to guide and inspire those who choose to lead from within. Rather than offering policy prescriptions or systematic reform strategies, leadership is the focus. I seek to inspire optimism and provide an example of what is possible when leaders take the lead on solving problems in any organization, no matter how daunting the task.

This book is not only for school leaders. It is intended for the public sector, nonprofits, and private businesses in need of turnaround leadership. I begin each chapter with a single word. Read it to yourself and then say it aloud with confidence. There is power in each of these words. Each word should remind you of an action, behavior, or mindset needed to lead a turnaround effort in any organization.

Then come along with me as I tackle real situations in my quest to keep my students and staff safe, and to educate them. Join me on my leadership journey, and learn why I answered the call to lead this persistently dangerous school when no one else would do so. Finally, discover why leadership makes all the difference when a school or company is off course.

As we take this journey together, I have included a section just for you at the end of each story: the "Thinking About Your Leadership" section. I would like for you to pause and reflect on "YOU" as the leader, just as I did before concluding each chapter.

This is the section where I wrote my story takeaways to help me focus my actions and behaviors as a leader. I have also included an "Examine Attentively" phrase that is a shorter version of my lesson takeaways for you to apply to your leadership mission. Read each word carefully and consider how you can use the word to guide your leadership. I also have included a "Questions for You" section. Sometimes reflection questions prompt more questions that could lead to answers in a particular situation. You may choose to read all three or just one reflection method. They are intended as a vehicle for us to take this leadership journey side by side, because, as you know, leadership can be lonely.

A final note: all of my stories are true, and some of my actions may not be typical. Leading a notorious persistently dangerous school called for unconventional tactics in order for my students, staff, and teachers to go home safely each night, and in order for my students to be educated. If you are faced with leading an organization in need of turnaround, make no apologies for your unconventional leadership, because I make no apologies for mine. As I always say, "If you are going to lead, you must LEAD." Lead boldly to reach your goals, and watch what you discover about yourself in the process.

# 1

# Envision

"**I** will take the blue one," I thought to myself. Prior to my start date, I was asked to select a chair for my new office. I decided on a beautiful, blue leather high back chair. At the time, I did not know why I selected the color blue. From what I could remember, every principal I ever had over my 20-year career always had a black chair. I had never seen a principal with a blue chair; yet somehow, I was drawn to the blue one. The moment I laid eyes on it, I knew there was something special about that blue chair. It was a different shade of blue, not ocean blue or royal blue, but a dull blue that stood out in the catalog. When the chair arrived, it was what I expected. It was comfortable, it made me feel important, and it gave off a sense of peace.

When I arrived to work at Fitzsimons High School early the morning of November 1, 2003, I sat in that blue chair. I started to wonder about my journey to this place, in this seat, and in this position—a principal with a big fancy office, a beautiful, blue leather chair, and a private bathroom. How did I get here? It was always my dream to be a great teacher, but being a principal far surpassed my vision of myself growing up poor in the same neighborhood where this school resided. Ironically, my grandmother owned a home directly across the street from Fitzsimons, and my family church, Trinity African Methodist Episcopal was on the corner. My family had belonged to that church for approximately 135 years.

Fitzsimons High School had changed over the years. It was once a junior high school. Then it became a middle school, and in 2002, it began its transformation into a gender-separate high school. It would have two separate schools in one building—one for young women, and one for young men. Each school would have its own principal. I was the principal for the young women at Fitzsimons.

I was feeling proud of myself when I was suddenly interrupted by girls screaming "Get her, get her!" followed by thumps, and then more thumps. I jumped up out of my chair and quickly opened my office door. I saw multiple girls and their families fighting each other. There were a lot of people fighting. Crazy fighting. . . . I could not believe it was girls, high school girls and women. It was like a gang fight, a street brawl, but it was inside of the school. Hair and blood were on the floor. It was a terrible sight. I quickly charged into the fight in an attempt to stop them from beating each other to death. In my effort to stop them from fighting, I grabbed the arm of one girl in the midst of her attempt to pound on another girl. She looked at me in a very hateful way and yelled, "Get the F--- off of me!" I did not release her right away. I held onto her arm firmly. She said again, "Get the F--- off of me." This time, I released my grip, because I thought to myself she must have me confused with someone else. Then I remembered that today was my first day as a principal, my first day as a principal ever. After working as a classroom teacher for 20 years, I had left to join Fitzsimons as a new teacher coach in September 2003. Two months later, I was named principal. My boss, Mr. Clayton, told me privately when he assigned me to Fitzsimons to be a teacher coach that there would be plenty of opportunities for advancement. I guess he was right.

How could she know that I was the principal?

After releasing my grip, I waited for the police to assist me in getting the fight under control. Once everything had calmed down, I announced for all the classes to come to the auditorium immediately. Before anything else could occur, I had to let the students and staff know that I was the new principal. Over the public address system, I asked every teacher to escort his or her classes to the auditorium. "Are you sure you want to do that?" asked one of the teachers. I did not answer her. I just made my way to the auditorium. As I stood on the stage, I could not believe my eyes. It looked like a scene from the movie *Lean on Me*, but worse. Students were running down the aisles and jumping over seats. The teachers did not know where their students were in the auditorium. The students were loud, using an excessive amount of profanity, and yelling at the teachers for trying to make them have a seat. They simply refused to be redirected. At that split second, I understood what the teacher was implying when she asked, "Are you sure you want do that?" By the way they entered the auditorium, you could tell that they had not been to the auditorium in a long time for any kind of meaningful program. The teachers, most of them first-year teachers, did not know what to do. They made no attempt to bring their students to order. They just stood, staring and waiting for the next huge fight to break out the way it had happened moments before near the main office. I froze, and stared out into the crowd from the stage. Holding the microphone, I murmured quietly, "What in the world did I get myself into?"

Instead of looking at the students, the teachers stared at me as if to say "She must be crazy for taking the job as principal." I wondered if any of them thought I was some sort of savior. Many of them seemed to want to burst into tears.

I focused my attention back to the students and tried to regain order in the room. I kept saying, "Young ladies! Young ladies, please take your seats." Using a demanding tone, I said, "Teachers, please stand near your children." I kept repeating that over and over until my voice echoed loudly over theirs. Then, in a harsh, bold tone this time, with my patience wearing thin, I said, "Sit down and close your mouths, or you will leave this auditorium and spend a few days at home with your parents." I did not know whether my tone or my threat got their attention. I signaled for the police to come into the room and remove anyone who would not sit down. Soon, the noise died down. There was still faint talking, but I could be heard over their voices. I said very loudly, boldly, and proudly to them all, "In case you do not know who I am, I am Mrs. Wayman, and I am your new principal." The children started to laugh and were totally uninterested by my announcement. They looked at me as if to say "So what?" The title "Principal" meant nothing to them. Why?

The teachers, on the other hand, did not know what to think. They had started the first two months without a principal, and because I had been working as a new teacher coach in the building, I knew they were accustomed to doing whatever they wanted to do, when they wanted to do it. While they were all still digesting the news that I was the new principal, I proceeded to list my expectations for their behavior and what they would learn in school. Then, suddenly, a young girl stood up in the rear of the auditorium and shouted, "Miss, Miss!" I tried to ignore her because she was yelling completely out of turn. She was loud and out of her seat. Despite my desire to ignore her for speaking out of turn, she continued to yell, "Miss, Miss!" Finally, our eyes locked. We stared at each other and she said again, "Miss, Miss!" this time adding, "Why do you keep calling this a school? **This is not a school**." I stood there speechless. I repeated her statement to myself over and over again. There it was, summed up in five words. This is not a school. That is what I was thinking when I walked up on the stage and looked into the audience. I could not figure out where I had seen this scene before. Then I remembered my own high school auditorium in 1976, in a school not too far from this one. That was when I first encountered the disparities in the educational system in Philadelphia for myself. We sat in the auditorium waiting to get our rosters and class assignments, and it was total chaos for a very long time. It was not what I was used to, coming from a school outside of the poverty-stricken area that I called home.

I quickly processed what she had shouted. (**This is not a school!**) Then, I responded by saying, "I am calling it a school because it is a school." She said, in a much softer, concerned voice, "No, it is not." I asked the young woman, "Then what is it, if it is not a school?" "Just a place to hang out," she replied.

Everyone started screaming and laughing in loud agreement. For them, school was a place to hang out. I digested this with horror. I wondered if they ever took the time to look around the neighborhood when they walked to school. Did they understand that a good education could improve their quality of life? Why couldn't they see opportunity in their school? Why were they unable to see their school as a school?

After that exchange, I sent everyone back to class. I returned to my office and sat in my new, blue leadership chair, and started asking myself some questions. Why did the word "Principal" mean nothing to them? Why did they see school as a place to hang out? More importantly, why did they not see that education could change their lives? I had so many questions that needed answers. As I sat in my blue leadership chair praying that another fight did not break out, I could not forget the young girl's question, "Why do you keep calling this a school?" More importantly, I could not forget how she answered her own question, "This is not a school."

I sat in that blue chair, and closed my eyes. There it was, the catalyst to all of the problems in the school: the reason for all of the violence; the reason for the school being given to an educational management company to manage for low academic performance; the reason why 70 percent of the teaching staff were a combination of first-year teachers or first-time teachers to the school; the reason why they could not find a principal, and solicited a new teacher coach to be principal in the middle of the school year. Fitzsimons was not a school.

The more I thought about it, the more outraged I became. I was mad at everybody: mad at the students for fighting; mad at their parents for helping them physically fight, but not fighting collectively for their children to be properly educated; mad at this place that had not been properly managed, so it had to be managed by outsiders; mad at the principals before me who allowed this place to get so out of control that the students now did not see it as a school. Then I remembered that I was the one who agreed to be the leader of this failing organization. I knew many of the facts before I consented to lead. I knew it was low-performing and dangerous, and I still chose to lead it. So, I realized that I had no one else to blame but myself for making it my responsibility to make this "place to hang out" into a school. The problem was now all mine. And I knew I had to save this organization because there was too much at stake. As a leader, I had to face the brutal fact that if I failed, hundreds of children would be uneducated and doomed to live in poverty. And if you had ever lived in poverty, as I had as a child, you would not want that life for anyone. So I made up my mind that I had to make that school a school.

A student created the vision for the school going forward on my first day as principal. It was my job as a leader to make that vision a reality.

## Thinking About Your Leadership

Clear vision and owning the responsibility to achieve that vision is the job of a turnaround leader. Before going into battle, a turnaround leader must know what he or she envisions for the organization before forming a shared vision.

**Examine Attentively:** Your vision for the organization you are leading.

**Questions for You:**
- What is *your* vision for the organization?
- Can you articulate it to others without hesitation?

# 2

# Discover

My vision was clear. I had to make the "place to hang out" into a school. To do that, I first needed to discover why exactly it wasn't a school. Let's remember what schools were intended to do: provide education and mental toughness so that children could live a long, happy life and contribute to the world around them in a very positive way. Schools were instituted to help poor children escape poverty. Public schools were formed by our forefathers to help level the playing field, so that we all could enjoy life and liberty, and pursue happiness.

For everyone else in that room, the student's comment meant nothing and they probably could not understand why I reacted so strongly to it. If you have ever been in a school that was not a school, then you would understand the pain of that comment. The statement cut though me like a knife. All the pain of attending an underperforming school in my neighborhood came rushing back. Why did I beg my mother to let me go there?

I knew the answer to my own question the moment I thought of it. I wanted to walk to school with my friends. I was tired of riding the bus to school for over an hour, only to wonder whether my sister and I would get home safely due to the racial tension in the northeast section (where I was being bussed as part of the district's desegregation program). That program had its challenges, but I soon discovered that what I had to endure from the educational system in my own neighborhood was far worse.

When the student said "This is not a school," I thought about all of the students in my class who could not read with fluency or read at all. When the teacher asked for volunteers to read, the room would grow silent—because everyone knew there were no volunteers. He would have to call on someone, and the thought of that happening left everyone paralyzed. How is it possible to go to school for nine years and not be able to read? I remembered wondering about this when I was in high school. I could still see many of my teachers sitting there reading their newspapers when they were supposed to be teaching. I thought about all the excessive talking by the students in the classroom when there was a teacher trying to teach. I remembered the teachers getting so fed up by the disrespect and the noise that they would sit down and tell us, "Okay, you do not want to listen? Fine, you just remember: I got mine, you have to get yours." That was the tagline every time they did not want to teach. "I got mine, you have to get yours." This was their abbreviated way of saying, "I have my education; you have to get your education." Get my education— from where, if not from the teacher? I thought about the large number of books copied from the duplicating machine because there were not enough copies to go around, just so we would have something to read. I thought about how difficult college was for me, and how close I came to failing because I did not learn all the content I was supposed to learn in high school that my roommate from another county in Pennsylvania had. I thought about my high school principal and wondered whether she knew that many of the teachers were not teaching. I never saw the principal in a classroom when I was in high school. Did she know that there were a few great teachers who tried to make a difference, but had a difficult time making up for lost years in our education?

I was the principal now. I wanted to know why these students, 36 years after my experience, felt that this was not a school.

So in the days that followed my first day as principal, I made it my business to find out. I was the leader with the vision, so I had to know fully what I was dealing with before I proceeded. I had to understand every area of this organization in order to make my vision a reality. I had to observe and make note of everything that needed fixing to make this school a school.

In my quest for understanding the source of the student's frustration, what I discovered was heartbreaking and unimaginable, even for me as a 20-year veteran teacher. I thought I had seen it all, until I saw it through the lens of a principal. The leader. The person responsible. I discovered a room with mirrors (and no, that's not a metaphor). I could not imagine what a school would need with a room full of mirrors. When I asked a staff member, she said, "Oh, that is the room where the students go to braid their hair when they are good in class." I was told that the previous principal knew about the room. The more I learned about the school, the more "Why do you keep calling this a school?" played over and over again in my mind.

I walked into a teacher's classroom to conduct an informal observation of her teaching practices. All of the desks were pushed to the back of the room and the students were jumping rope. When I asked her why they were jumping rope, she told me that it was a math lesson. I'm sure there are ways to use activities like jumping rope in math lessons, but I didn't think that was the case here. So I asked her to show me the lesson plan that called for jumping rope. She did not have such a plan. I flashed back to my college days once more as I put an immediate end to the rope jumping. I thought about being tutored around the clock when I was failing math, because I had never seen that content before. My roommate would say, "Linda, you should have learned this in high school." I never saw any of it in high school. (Why do you keep calling this a school?)

When I questioned the teachers about their lesson plans, one of them said, "I was told nothing. I asked the principal specifically about lesson plans, and she just looked at me like that was a bizarre question." The teachers' contract requires that teachers prepare weekly plans. I thought about my years in the classroom and I remember being asked to write lesson plans, but they were only reviewed when I was formally observed. I only remember receiving feedback on them a few times in 20 years. How would the principal know what and how the teachers were teaching if they never reviewed the teachers' lesson plans? Detailed lesson plans with clear goals in mind are the foundation for successful student learning. Lesson plans assure that time is used wisely, all standards are taught, student needs are met, and knowledge is acquired. Lesson plans are most effective when they are well thought out in writing, reviewed, implemented as written, revised if needed, include differentiation strategies, and include an assessment that is tied to the learning objective. At Fitzsimons, lesson planning did not happen. No planning equaled no progress! (Why do you keep calling this a school?)

It was approaching the time for report card conferences, and I noticed I had a stack of report cards that did not have grades on them. I called one teacher into my office to ask him why his grades were not on the report card. He responded in a very nasty tone that they weren't submitted because he did not have a computer in his classroom. I reminded him that there were several computer labs in the school, to which he responded, "When you put a computer in my room, I will give them grades." (Why do you keep calling this a school?)

There were no individual rosters for the students, so they traveled in cohorts like elementary school children. They received English instruction for 110 minutes for only half the year, when most of the students could not read or write proficiently. An entire roster had to be built from scratch. So every student and teacher received a new roster mid-year. It was the right thing to do. (Why do you keep calling this a school?)

There was no system for discipline in place. The students did what they wanted to do. The students did not respect the teachers, and many of the teachers did not respect the students. There were no activities going on in the school. It was just chaos at every turn.

*Why do you keep calling this a school?*

Now that I had discovered so many examples that caused confusion in the minds of the students, I had tangible reasons why, in their eyes, this was not a school. It was time to act.

## Thinking About Your Leadership

Organizations that are failing need turnaround leaders. They lead the charge to take the organization in a positive direction. Discover all or most of the challenges before proceeding. It is best to conduct your own investigation. Act on any challenge that needs immediate attention. You are the leader. You have the vision. Before attacking the challenges, you must observe, make notes, think, and remember what is at stake.

**Examine Attentively:** All the challenges in every area of your organization, then act.

**Questions for You:**

- Knowing your present organization's challenges, can you visualize where you want the organization to be at the end of *your* term as leader?
- Are you prepared to ask the hard questions about the organization and to hear the real answers?

# 3

# Select

Leading is very difficult. At the beginning of this transformation effort, I felt alone. But I knew it was my purpose, and I knew what was at stake; and those two understandings kept me focused. I was determined not to fail. I could not fail.

After discovering and documenting all of the challenges involved in making Fitzsimons a better school, I set out to correct each and every one of them. I separated my challenges into three categories: building relationships; teaching and learning; and school safety.

I worked as hard as I could to rectify the problems that stood in the way of reaching my goal, but I was keenly aware that I had to create a leadership team if real sustainable change was going to happen. It was impossible to do alone. I needed the support of my own team. Sure, there was a leadership team in place when I entered Fitzsimons, but it was not *my* team. So I started to build a team one selection at a time. I had to enter the new school year armed with what and whom I needed to succeed.

To find the right members for my team, I made it my job to observe everyone as often as I could. I did not care about their job titles. Titles meant absolutely nothing to me. I was more concerned with their aptitude for growth, and their commitment to the students.

I set aside large chunks of time to sit in every classroom and record what I heard and saw. I listened to the words the teachers used. Were those words positive or negative? Did they make the students feel important through their actions and words? Did they hold the students accountable for their actions? Did they teach their content well? Were they having fun with the students? What did their classrooms look like? Were they bright and cheerful? Did they have positive sayings on the wall? Were the sayings posted relevant to the children they taught? Did they seem to love their students, and did they seem to love to teach? I did not concern myself with the years of teaching experience. As stated earlier, many of them were first-year teachers. I was observing for potential. I was looking for a turnaround leadership team.

After observing the teachers, I observed the support staff completing their work. What skills could they bring to the leadership table? I carried a desk and a chair, took piles of papers and my computer, and sat in the hallway of a different floor each day to complete my central office work. I would sit there all day observing and taking notes. I would also always have my walkie-talkie with me. I would turn it up very high so that I could hear what was happening in other parts of the building. I wanted to hear the conversations going on everywhere. What I heard would give me a good feeling or a bad feeling about what was going on with the support staff in that building. I went to the lunchroom every day and monitored how the food was served to the children. I listened to the conversations as they served them. Did the cafeteria workers smile at the students when they fed them or did they just throw the food onto plates? I observed it all.

Before making my final selection, I thought of people who were in my life outside of the school. Did any of them possess special qualities and skills that could support my vision? I was looking everywhere for a turnaround team, and the members had to have special qualities in order to do this difficult work, including commitment, love for their work, skill in their chosen areas, and an aligned reason for doing the work. They had to see it the way I did, as lifesaving work. They had to understand poverty and all of its symptoms. They had to understand that the students needed support. They had to understand that some of the students' actions were simply cries for help. They had to have hope for what was possible, even in this bleak situation.

After my observing period was over, I selected the first three members of my team. Each selection was made with a particular purpose in mind.

The first person I selected was Mr. Mike Spangenberg. He was an English teacher. There were many reasons why he was my first selection for the team. He was smart and committed to getting the very best out of every one of his students. He was never afraid, and he cared about everyone, even me.

I will never forget in the spring of my first year as principal when a group of guys and girls from a street gang came to the school to fight my young ladies. I forced them to stay inside the building because I was told there were weapons involved. I had to do my best to convince them of the potential dangers in order to get the students to stay inside the building and not to confront the gang. They stayed inside only because I begged them not to leave. My girls wanted to fight the gang, but they did not want me to worry. They had started to care about me right before my eyes.

In my frustration, I proceeded to walk down the long street just to talk to the gang members. All of the neighbors at this time were hanging out of the top windows of their two-story homes to see what was happening, and crowds were beginning to form on the street. They were getting prepared to see the action; they hadn't bothered to call the cops. Not that it would have mattered. When my secretary called the police station, she was told that it was shift change time and no one could come right away. Shift change? There was about to be a gang fight, and it was shift change time, so no cops were available. This happened almost every day at dismissal.

As I continued down the street, I could hear the voice of an older woman screaming out her window saying, "Miss, Miss, go back! Go back, Miss, they are dangerous. Go back, please." She was begging me to turn back—but I thought that if I could just talk to the gang members I could get them to leave, so that I could send my students home. Despite the warning scream from the window, I kept walking toward the gang. Then suddenly, I felt someone come up alongside of me. We started to walk lockstep together. It was Mr. Spangenberg. I yelled at him to return to the school several times, but he would not turn back. As we walked side by side, getting closer and closer to the gang, I remembered that this young man was barely 22 years old. He was right out of college. He was born and raised far away from Philadelphia. He was from Minnesota. What did he know about all of this craziness?

I stopped in the middle of the block, halfway between the gang and the school where my students were being held hostage, and told him once more to go back to the school. He refused. "If you are going to go down there," he said, "I will have to go with you." In that instant, I remembered meeting his parents. And I thought to myself that I could not let anything happen to him. I had promised them that. So, very reluctantly, I retreated back to the school and away from the gang. As we were walking back, the new shift of police finally arrived. They dispersed the gang, and I was able to release my students.

That single incident taught me that Mr. Spangenberg understood my vision and my purpose. He could see the potential of every student, and he cared about me.

Mr. Spangenberg was my first leadership team member. He earned the title "first follower." I did not ask him to be a part of the team; I told him he was a part of the team. I walked right up to him and said, "You are going to be our new school scheduler." I needed someone to rebuild the school schedule as if this was a brand-new school. When he replied that he didn't know anything about how to build a schedule, I responded by saying, "So what. You are smart. You can learn anything." After that day, I was no longer alone in this turnaround effort. It was Mr. Spangenberg, the vision, and me, as we went to work to make this school a school.

I went on to name a second teacher to the leadership team— Ms. Jennifer Speirs. She was also an English teacher. What a magnificent teacher! She was born and raised in Florida, and you could see her smile from a mile away. It was infectious. She always smiled and had a positive thing to say to everyone, especially her students. Ms. Speirs would refer to her students as "scholars." When she met them for the first time she gave them pencils with taped-on tags that read, "Scholars work hard, scholars succeed, we are scholars." I remember the first day she called them scholars. They all turned and looked at each other. Then one girl said, "What is a scholar?" Ms. Speirs told them her definition for scholar: a student, a learner, and an intellectual. "You are a scholar," she continued. "Each and every one of you is meant to do great things in this world, but it takes hard work! Scholars work hard. Scholars succeed. You are a scholar. During this course, you will be expected to work hard and use your voice to make the world a better place. You will be successful. You are a scholar when you enter this room." These students had never been told that they were important in such a powerful and delightful way. They responded to her smile and her expectations because they knew she loved them and believed in what they could become. Ms. Speirs demonstrated that this school could really be a school if I could just get the other teachers to see it her way.

I placed Ms. Speirs on the leadership team because she was positive, intelligent, and made everyone feel hopeful. Ms. Speirs was the second person on the leadership team because she was also a believer in my "why" for the work. And she simply loved being a teacher.

Rounding out the third and final spot in my newly formed leadership team was Ms. Annetta Jackson. I first met Ms. Jackson at her home prior to becoming a principal. I worked with her children in a variety of ways. We would sit and talk after my sessions with her children. I told her that I admired her organizational skills. Everything in her home was very well organized.

When I became a principal, I immediately thought of Ms. Jackson and her amazing ability to organize. I approached Ms. Jackson and asked her to come and work with me at Fitzsimons. She agreed to come, but the problem was that the only available position was on the young men's side of the building, which had its own principal. When our paths would cross daily, I would see her constantly taking notes and trying to remember all of the students by name. The young men were 100 percent more challenging than the young women, and Ms. Jackson was just trying to keep it all together. Seeing Ms. Jackson daily reinforced my resolve to make the school a school, even though only the young women were my responsibility.

As I prepared for the new school year, I budgeted for a new position titled Noon Time Aid. Ms. Jackson would work side by side with me in this position. She was a pillar of strength.

She wanted things to be right in the world and always did her part to make life better for others. She was a giver, she was loyal, and she was skilled with a talent that would prove to be very valuable. With her organizational skills and my vision, I was sure that we would begin to make our mark on making the school a school.

I sat in my blue leadership chair thinking about my challenges, my bright spots, and my selections. I had my purpose, my vision, and my challenges etched in my mind; and now I had people who believed in my vision. I had people who could help me improve the three major categories that would enhance the school experience for many young women: building relationships; teaching and learning; and school safety. Individually we had our own strengths, but together, we formed a stronger team.

## Thinking About Your Leadership

Own that leading a turnaround effort is difficult and at times lonely. Record all of the challenges—and the bright spots—in the organization. Think about ways to address them, and solve as many as you can until the time comes to search for members of your turnaround team. Observe everything you can about them yourself. Do not get caught up in the titles of the employees. Locate the best workers with the skills you need to succeed. Assemble a top-notch leadership team that believes in your reason for doing the work and your vision for the future. Let your "why" and their "why" intersect. Then you will have a leadership team that will make a difference.

**Examine Attentively:** How you select members for your leadership team.

**Questions for You:**
- How will you find members of your turnaround leadership team?
- Can you identify the skills, talents, and mindset needed from each team member in order to form a great leadership team?

# 4

# Adapt

As we prepared to leave for the Christmas holiday break, I sat in my blue leadership chair and reflected on all of the challenges and rewards I had encountered. The first half of my first year as principal was almost over. The young women were a little more settled now thanks to a focus on building relationships, teaching and learning, and school safety.

The leadership team had set their sights on improving the conditions for the upcoming school year. They were working diligently on the school's schedule, culture, safety procedures, and instructional mandates. Introducing new systems in November was difficult to do. Nevertheless, we started to pilot many of these ideas before the holiday break, to see whether they would improve the overall culture of the school. We continued to pilot these ideas after the holiday break, so that we would have data to support our ideas before they became a part of a permanent plan. In addition to putting schoolwide rules and consequences in place, we also developed a system to monitor and implement the schoolwide behavior system. We insisted that the teachers write and submit lesson plans. I reviewed them and provided feedback. Classroom observations were held often. And I delivered frequent professional development training to assist the teachers in enhancing their instructional practices.

We worked very hard to build relationships with the students by having fun with them. We had school dances, held project fairs, took many field trips, and planned barbeques for the staff and students. We even went on retreats, so that we could provide quality time for us to get to know each another. And we often stayed very late, just to sit around and talk with them—and push them to dream past what they could see in North Philadelphia.

Intense daily focus on building relationships, teaching and learning, and school safety led to an increased workload for many teachers. We would often hear them say, "This is just too much work." Many could not wait until the school year ended so that they could move on. That was the best decision for the school, and for the students. Working in a turnaround situation takes dedication, strength, and buy-in. Without those three elements, it can seem like "too much work." With the majority of teachers who made the decision to leave, I gave them my blessing. But if there was a teacher I felt the students needed, I would call these teachers into my office, have heart-to-heart conversations, and try to convince them to stay. Sometimes it worked and sometimes it did not, but I owed it to the children to try. The teachers who wanted to stay were special beyond measure. They never thought that saving the lives of children was too much work.

I did not get a lot of private time during the school day. When I did get a few moments to myself, I always went back to my blue chair to relax, think, and brainstorm solutions to the many problems happening in the school. Students often interrupted my private moments. However, one day I was interrupted by a district official along with the head of the Educational Management Organization (EMO). They had come to inform me that the principal on the young men's side of the building would not be returning to complete the school year. That made me instantly very sad. I liked and respected the young men's principal. He used to walk me to my car every night long past the time for dismissal, long after we had discussed what went on in the building. We spent a lot of time each day trying to keep the young men and young women on their designated sides of the building. The young men's principal and I had different leadership styles, but we respected each other's work.

I continued to sit in my chair, listening to what they had to say and feeling very sad. The head of the EMO said that they needed time to find a suitable replacement. Then there was a long pause before he announced that they were not going to replace him for the remainder of the school year. I sat up in my chair because I thought I knew what he was going to say next: "Mrs. Wayman, we need you to be the principal of the young women's side of the building *and* the young men's side of the building." I stared at them in shock, trying to process what I was hearing. I was a first-year principal. The young women were tough, but the young men seemed even more impossible to handle. I had great relationships with some of them, but we only interacted when I pleaded with them to stay on their side of the school. How was I supposed to run two troubled schools? I already had to deal with massive fighting, minimal instruction, disengaged teachers, violent teachers, braiding rooms, rope jumping in the classroom, and no school vision—and now I had to deal with double the amount of problems? I had never heard of any principal running two separate schools in one building. As I sat in my blue leadership chair trying to think about the correct thing to say, I came to a quick decision. "I am not going to run two schools in one building," I blurted out. "I am going to run one school in one building. I will merge them as one school for the remainder of the year." I sat back in my chair and waited for a response. There was none. They were so overwhelmed by the challenge and circumstances surrounding the young men not having a principal that they did not care about the lead I was taking. They just wanted to get through the rest of the school year.

Since the school year was half over, I left the school gender-separate. That was the EMO's vision, but I did merge the staff. They had to conform to all of the directives I had already given to the teachers on the young women's side of the building. That did not go over well. They were never required to write and submit lesson plans, they were never observed and given written feedback, they did not have a schoolwide behavior system that was working, and they did not focus on having fun in conjunction with learning. They did not have a vision to make their school a school. But I did. And merging the two schools for the remainder of the school year was the right thing to do.

The next couple of months would be dedicated to changing the landscape of the entire building. There would be no more your-side, my-side. We had to come together as a staff in one building, with one principal. We had to notify the parents and the young men. The only way to ease the tensions with the young men was to build relationships with them by first respecting them. They were big on respect. I knew I had made that a reality before we formally joined as a school just by speaking to them, redirecting them, and being courteous to them as I traveled throughout the building. But being their principal was going to be a different story.

When we returned from the Christmas holiday break, we were one school.

On that day, I witnessed the power of relationship building with the young men. The young men had decided to have an unconventional snowball fight outside the school at dismissal. They were not just throwing snow; they were throwing ice balls. Many students were getting hit and hurt. After the gang incident, I always made it a point to go outside at dismissal to say good-night and send my students home safely. When I saw what was going on, I ran into the corner store for cover, and assessed what I was dealing with. There were a lot of young men throwing ice. I was the only adult outside. And without a walkie-talkie, I could not call for assistance. There were just too many children for me to approach by myself, so I stayed inside the store. If it had been my young ladies, I would have walked up to them and told them to stop; but I did not know many of the young men outside, and many of them did not go to Fitzsimons.

The store's owner knew I was the principal and assisted me in calling the police. Not surprisingly, I got the same response we got during the gang incident: "It is shift change time. We will send someone after the shift officially changes." I wanted them to stop throwing the ice. So I decided to go outside and try to do what I could to get them to stop. But the store's owner stopped me and asked if I had any children. I responded by saying, "Yes, two daughters." He said, "Well then, do not go out there until you get some help, for your children's sake." When he said that, I instantly thought about who would take care of my children if I was killed by an ice ball. The thought of that reality forced me to stay in the store. I wanted to stop them from potentially hurting each other, yet I realized it was extremely dangerous.

As I stood in the store waiting for the ice throwing to cease, a young man walked into the store. He was a student at Fitzsimons. It was rumored that he was selling drugs and had access to dangerous weapons. I had seen him in the school, but I had never spoken with him personally. "Mrs. Wayman, what are you doing in here?" he asked. I told him that I came into the store to avoid being hit with the ice, and that when the fighting got worse I had called the police. I told him that I loved them all, but also had two children at home who needed their mother. He looked at me and smiled. "Mrs. Wayman, no one is going to hit you." "Son, I do not know that," I responded. "All I know is that at my age if I get hit in the head with ice, it could kill me." Then he put out his hand. "Take my hand, and I will walk you across the street. No one will hit you for sure." He was so sure of himself that I allowed a 15-year-old child to hold my hand and walk me outside the store and across the street to the school building. The craziest thing happened. Suddenly, I was no longer afraid. I did not know why. He was a child to me. I grabbed his hand and walked outside, where they were still throwing ice. Then the young man holding my hand said in a loud, commanding voice, "Not one piece of ice better hit Miss Wayman or me." He only had to say it once. The ice throwing immediately stopped. I could not believe that one young man had all that power. He walked me safely back to the door of the school, holding hands the whole way, and the entire snowball fight came to an end. He was my guardian angel. When we released our hands, I said, "Thank you. Thank you very much." He never responded. He just walked off.

When I saw him in school the next day, I thanked him again. Then I said to him, "Son, you were born to lead." He smiled and said "I know!" I begged him to stay in school, but shortly after the episode he left school and I never saw him again. I was told he went to prison for gun-related charges. It broke my heart to think of someone with such leadership abilities locked behind bars. It only made me want to save the children even more. I was often reminded of what was at stake if I could not make school a viable option for them. The only way to do that now was not only to make one school a school, but to make two schools one school. This situation taught me that adolescents watch and study adults, even when we do not watch and study them. The young man who helped me had respect for me and knew the others wouldn't harm me because of the way I had treated them. Relationship building is a major key in doing away with persistently dangerous schools.

There were six months remaining in the school year. I could have just let it ride with one side of the building doing one thing and the other side doing another, but I could not do that because the young men's side was even less of a school than the young women's side. The young men were completely out of control all school year, even though the principal had worked himself to death to make it right. The main problem with the young men was just getting them into the classroom. Now that, on top of everything else, had become my problem.

I had never heard of a school merging in the entire 20 years I was teaching in the district.

I worked hard to hold the entire building together for the rest of the school year. The three people I had identified to be on the leadership team were mainly focused on the 2004–2005 school year. We wanted to start that year off perfectly. This sudden major happening threw us all for a loop. We made a few adjustments to the young men's master schedule to blend with ours. And the staff on the young men's side had to conform to our way of doing things in order to move the entire school closer to the vision.

At the end of the 2003–2004 school year, we breathed a sigh of relief. We had made it. And what was most impressive was that the school actually managed to make some academic gains amidst all of the challenges. We learned a lot from the merger of the school mid-year. To name a few, we learned that people have to buy into a vision for it to work. They have to be committed to seeing the change they want to see. And they have to be willing to do the extra work to make it happen. But what we learned the most from the merger was that two schools in one building was not going to work. Having two different principals in one building with two separate visions was hard enough to do in a turnaround situation. In order to make it a school, it had to have one vision with one leader.

The EMO took their concerns to the district officials, who agreed to allow the creation of two separate schools—one for the young men, and one for the young women. To make this happen, a second merger would have to take place.

Fitzsimons High School would merge by gender with Rhodes High School, another high school in North Philly that was being managed by the same EMO. The young women from both schools would occupy the Rhodes building, forming a new school called "The Young Women's Leadership School at Rhodes." The young men from both schools would be in the Fitzsimons building, forming the "The Young Men's Leadership School at Fitzsimons." I would be the principal of the Young Women's Leadership School at Rhodes. We would have a full school year to plan, since we were scheduled to move into our new location in July 2005. But this would not be an easy merger, because the young women in these two schools were rivals in every sense of the word. We had a lot to do to in preparation for merger number two.

It was June 30, 2005, my last day at Fitzsimons High School. I sat in my blue leadership chair and thought about all of the times I returned to that chair, crisis after crisis, trying to figure out a solution. That chair was the only tangible thing I had to lean on when I was lonely in my office, but determined to lead. For some reason it gave me the strength I needed. I often ask myself why an ordinary chair became such a personal symbol of strength. Why did I always seem to come up with a solution or deal with horrific problems successfully when I sat in that chair? Why did that chair mean so much to me? Why did I take to the chair so seriously?

When I packed up all my belongings to relocate to Rhodes with my young women, the last thing that I packed was my blue leadership chair. I was told that there was already a principal's chair at Rhodes, but I told everyone that the blue chair would have to come with me. On that day I decided that the blue leadership chair would be the only leadership chair I would ever own. It would always travel with me whenever I was called to lead. I placed it carefully near my other belongings for pick-up by the district movers.

I arrived at Fitzsimons as principal with an unclear vision and left with a vision that was forever etched into my mind:

Create schools that provide children with the means to end poverty.

To reach that goal, it would take leadership.

## Thinking About Your Leadership

Change happens suddenly and often in turnaround efforts. But nothing should take you off course to completion of your final mission. You may have to adapt and change course, but always remember what is at stake: a vision becoming reality. This must be the motivating factor to keep you on course.

As you move toward the final goal, there will be people and situations that will remind you "why" you must do what you are doing. Learn from them. The reminder may come from an unlikely source. Trust the source of your "reminder." It can be very authentic, but not obvious. It may be a test. Positive relationship building is a must to bring about change.

**Examine Attentively:** Your ability to adapt and lead when sudden change occurs.

**Questions for You:**

- Can you lead boldly in times of sudden change?
- Can you learn valuable lessons to improve your leadership from people you may only encounter once in your lifetime?

# 5

# Synthesize

The Fitzsimons leadership team prepared throughout the entire 2004–2005 school year to merge the young women from Fitzsimons and Rhodes. We grew from a team of four to a dream team of nine, adding an assistant principal, three additional teachers, and a college-bound counselor. Each of them had exceptional skills and a clear reason for believing in the change effort.

Working all day and planning to go into Rhodes all night left me at times discouraged about the daunting journey. In order to get the team ready for the amount of work ahead, and to ease their fears and concerns, I felt compelled to describe my role as leader on the team. I gently explained to them that leadership is a calling, an assignment that I take very seriously. I told them that true leaders do not delegate their work; they are visible, reliable, and serve as thought partners with the team. True leaders accept the blame if failure happens, without excuses, and share success with the team. It would always be my job to stay in the loop in every area of the organization, to push them to take risks if it was good for the children, to inspire them to do their best work, and to celebrate them when it was time for them to move on. I emphasized that I was willing to lead, and willing to work hard. I wanted to remove the stress of them thinking that they were all alone in their work. After I had finished speaking, I saw the relief on their faces. We quickly forged ahead with the planning of our entrance into the Young Women's Leadership School at Rhodes.

For months, we took time to dissect all of the notes I had compiled during my year of observations at Fitzsimons. When we were finished analyzing the notes, we researched best practices to make sure we were concentrating in the areas that needed the most attention. We read books, watched videos, and told many stories about our interactions with the students and their families, teachers, and staff—compiling lots and lots of information in the process. In the end, when it was time to solidify our plan of action to enter Rhodes successfully, we concluded that we would continue to focus our attention on the same three areas that led to the improvements at Fitzsimons: building relationships, teaching and learning, and school safety. We believed that if we could find new ways to build positive relationships with the students and staff, get all the educators to discover the art of teaching so that the students could learn, and make the school a safe place, we could indeed make Rhodes a great high school for girls.

The rest of the leadership team had made several trips to Rhodes to prepare for our move. At every leadership team meeting they would give a report, and every report painted an even more somber picture. They reported that the teachers were mean to them when they visited; that they did not see much teaching going on; that the students displayed severe behavior problems; and that even though the principal hadn't left yet, the two assistant principals were the only people visible at all times, and they were putting out fires as they happened in the school. They never had the opportunity to speak with the current principal and added that they rarely saw him.

In order to avoid major clashes between the two sets of young women, it was the responsibility of the counselor of both schools to hold interest sessions with the girls and try to iron out any potential problems. Rumors were flying that the two groups did not like each other and did not want the schools to merge. The young women from these two schools were known to fight often. Schools in North Philadelphia are territorial, and the young women from Fitzsimons were going to have to cross territory lines to get to Rhodes. That was cause for concern. The team pressed on in trying to communicate with the staff and students at Rhodes, but they worried that merging might not be a good idea. After every report, I reminded them of our mission, and of our determination to make it work. We could not stay at Fitzsimons. We had to leave. We had to be successful. I told them that we were on the brink of something groundbreaking. We could not be deterred.

On July 1, 2005, I walked into The Young Women's Leadership School at Rhodes for the first time as principal. With all of the negative news on my mind, the first item of business was to find my new principal's office to see whether my blue leadership chair had arrived. I smiled when I saw it waiting behind the new desk where it belonged.

I set my things down on my desk and prepared to walk the entire building. I needed to see the layout and get the feel of the building. The school was a massive structure—a far cry from the building size at Fitzsimons. The merger of the two schools at Rhodes was twice the size of the merger at Fitzsimons. This merger involved the merging of two teaching and support staffs, two student populations, and two communities. It entailed creating a brand-new, all-girls' high school in the middle of North Philadelphia. Sure, there were other private high schools for girls, catholic high schools for girls, charter schools for girls, and even a renowned public high school for girls (with strict entrance requirements), but what was going to make Rhodes special was that it would be a neighborhood school. There would be NO entrance requirement. You only had to live in the North Philadelphia neighborhood and be female. No lotteries, picking, selecting, or rejecting was allowed.

As I walked alone through the building for the first time, I recalled not having this opportunity when I became the principal of Fitzsimons. I had been familiar with the building, but had not looked at it through the lens of a principal. As I walked from room to room, I could not believe what I was witnessing. There were literally thousands of books thrown on the floor in several classrooms. The floors were cluttered with debris. I asked the cleaning staff about their timetable for getting the rooms clean and in proper order. One responded by saying, "When you pick up the books, we will clean the floors. It is not in our contract to pick up books." When *I* pick up the books? I was the principal. It may not be in your contract to pick up the books, I thought to myself, but this is a school—and children would be there in two months! I walked away from them while they stood there, looking down at the pile of books and refusing to pick them up.

I walked out of the classroom and turned the corner into the library. It appeared as if someone had taken a hammer to every piece of library furniture. Chopped-up wood was scattered all over the floor. You could not distinguish the desks from the chairs. It was just piles and piles of broken wood. My mouth opened wide in disbelief. Who would do such a thing!

The teachers who departed the school because of the merger never touched a thing in their classrooms. It seemed as if they had just picked up their personal items and left. There were walls that had been knocked down, and other walls with big holes in them. Somebody had made it his or her personal business to destroy the facility. People who love children would never have turned a building to ruins. It was deliberate. It was mean.

The sitting principal never once reached out to see whether there was anything I needed. But what he did do, which turned out to be his biggest gift to me, was allow me to complete the Rhodes budget for the 2005–2006 school year prior to becoming principal. That was very important, because I did not have to live with his decisions during my first year at Rhodes. That had been one of my major problems at Fitzsimons, trying to run a school with a vision of another principal. This time, I made all of the major decisions prior to going into the school.

After seeing the physical building conditions, speaking with the custodial staff, and recalling the leadership team reports, I remembered why I had put so much energy into learning all of the union contracts. I read them all line by line. When I wanted a way to bring my staff from Fitzsimons to Rhodes, I turned to the union contract to give me a solution. When I wanted to know what the custodial staff could and could not do, I turned to the union contract. When I wanted to know procedures for everything, I turned to the union contract. When I could not find a reference in a contract to a practice I wanted to mandate, that meant it was allowed. Contracts are up to interpretation, and I always pushed that interpretation to favor what was needed for children. Knowing the contracts gave me the information I needed to get what I wanted done. At times my staff tried to use it against me in order to avoid adhering to certain requests, and I used it as evidence that they must.

After completing my tour of the building and heading back to my office, I ran into the building engineer. He was quick to tell me about his relationship with the previous principal, and we struck up a positive conversation. He could see the disgust on my face at what I'd seen in the school, and said, "Mrs. Wayman, this school did not have to be run so poorly. I attended this school many years ago and it was not like this. I know I am only the building engineer, but can I give you one tip on how to manage this school?" When I said yes, he explained, "When I went here we did not use all of these staircases. We only used one. May I show you?" He walked me to the one staircase. "You can get everywhere in this building by just using this one staircase. You do not have to use all eight." I thanked him for the tip and went back to my office. I recorded that information into a small notebook and jotted down all that I had witnessed on my tour.

Then I picked up my purse and car keys, glanced at my blue leadership chair, and drove myself to the nearest hospital. I entered the emergency room with severe chest pains. I thought I was having a heart attack. As I lay on the bed in the hospital alone, I again remembered the student's words, "This is not a school." I remembered analyzing the state testing data from Rhodes, which revealed that only 3 percent of the students were proficient in math, and 9 percent in English. I remembered that I would be bringing that student, as well as nearly 300 of my other young women from Fitzsimons, and I did not want them to say those five words to me again on their first day at Rhodes. So, as I lay there, I promised God that I would make Rhodes into a School.

Thankfully, I did not have a heart attack. Instead, I was diagnosed with an anxiety attack and released from the hospital. I never told my family, and went to work the next day ready for the hard work ahead.

## Thinking About Your Leadership

When leading a turnaround mission, prepare yourself. Do your homework. Research, read, take notes, listen, and learn. When it is time to produce a final plan of action, synthesize all the information you have gathered and be prepared to use it to create a plan of action. Know who is supposed to be doing what, and use all you have learned to get others to work to their full capacity. Speak to anyone who may have previous knowledge of the organization and can give you valuable tips. Lead by example. Be present. Be in it.

**Examine Attentively:** Your ability to combine multiple sources of information to devise a winning plan.

**Questions for You:**

- Did you seek to gather all pertinent information about your organization before making a final decision on the plan for success?

- Do your employees see you in the battle to win the war with them?

# 6

# Rollout

Before the doors opened for students at Rhodes in September 2005, my team and I picked up every book and every piece of broken furniture so that the cleaning staff could clean the building. It turned out that, although picking up the books and the debris was not their responsibility, cleaning the school until it was spotless was their responsibility. And that's what they did.

The leadership team had a plan to make the Young Women's Leadership School at Rhodes a great school. We were all very well aware that the initial rollout of the plan would be key to the success of our overall vision of helping children escape poverty. The Rhodes transformation plan was a continuation of the Fitzsimons transformation plan. It was just much more refined, and we had evidence that we were building a winning formula. Building relationships, teaching and learning, and school safety remained our three areas of focus.

Building relationships was at the center of everything. It was purposely intertwined throughout every decision made. Clear, frequent, and sometimes dramatic communication with the students and staff would be necessary in building trust and positive relationships. The plan called for us to meet every student where they were emotionally and academically and encourage them to be their best with our help. We would have open and honest communication with them on all topics; be consistent in what we were asking them to do; be relentless in our expectations of them socially and academically; take frequent outings with them; participate in what mattered to them; always listen and question them; and always be sure to call them by name when we encountered them. It was our belief that building positive relationships would be the foundation of our success.

The first day of professional development with the merged staff at Rhodes was in late August, before the students were to arrive in September. It was time to roll out the plan the leadership team had worked on for over a year. When I walked into the lunchroom where the meeting was being held, you could cut the tension with a knife. The staff that followed from Fitzsimons to Rhodes was excited for the challenge. However, the staff that remained at Rhodes was unfriendly and at times rude. The rollout plan would be new for them, so I think they were just bracing themselves.

I opened our first professional development session together with a short summary of my past. I told them with every ounce of passion I had about growing up in poverty, not getting a real high school education, and going to college with what amounted to an eighth-grade education. I explained that my high school teachers never prepared me for college. Then I told them about the teachers who were exceptions, teachers who tried to fill the holes in my education but fell short because they ran out of time.

I told them my vision for the students at Rhodes High School: to have as many children escape poverty as possible. I emphasized that the only way for that to happen is to have an education. I told the teachers that it was my expectation that they would teach to the best of their ability every day, and I reminded the support staff that they were there to do just that: support the teachers in every way possible. I needed them to see it from my lens before I started my explanation of the teaching and learning system. I needed my vision to be clearly communicated. It was going to be massive work, and I needed to set the stage for why it must be done.

To begin the rollout of the teaching and learning system, I held up a copy of the teachers' contract. I could see the surprise in their eyes when I asked them to follow along as I explained the collective bargaining structure used for the foundation and installation of the new instructional program. (I would have read it to them, but that is against union rules.) What I needed as a guide to get the students to proficiency was right there in print. The contract outlined the following:

> The preparation of a daily or weekly lesson plan outline by a teacher is **required**. The lesson plan outline shall include: the **daily activities** of the class including **topic, instructional goals, instructional strategies, resources/materials and supplies and references to textbooks and curriculum guides**. Each teacher shall have available emergency lesson plans for use by substitutes. If a teacher's performance appears to be, or is becoming **unsatisfactory, he/she may be required to prepare more detailed lesson plans.**[*]

This passage in the contract was the engine behind the instructional transformation.

I wanted to introduce my system in this dramatic way because I did not want the same backlash I had received from the teachers at Fitzsimons when I asked them to prepare a weekly lesson plan. I wanted the teachers to know before the school doors opened that I was fully aware of what they were expected to do, with the approval of their union. I wanted to take the union card out of play right away, because it was the card that almost caused the system to fall apart at Fitzsimons. I had seen it happen many times throughout my long career.

This contractual obligation required a lot from the teachers, and I was determined to have them comply. The children needed them to comply in order to learn. After watching the Rhodes teachers reading this passage, I could only assume that they never complied with it. Why? Because they were never required to.

---

[*]"PFT-District Collective Bargaining Agreement, 2009-2013," Philadelphia Federation for Teachers, August 2012, www.pft.org/pft-contract.

From my teacher training, I knew that teacher planning was the catalyst for student learning, so I needed the lesson plans to be of substance. The contract outlined all the substance that was needed for student learning. I needed the teachers to coordinate what their students should know and be able to do inside and outside the classroom. It would all begin with effective lesson planning.

The teachers were informed that they would submit their lesson plans to the main office every Tuesday for the following week. It was the secretary's job to receive the plans and indicate that they were submitted. It they were not submitted by the deadline, the teachers would have to tell the administration why the directive was not followed. The assistant principal and I would read each and every plan, and give our written feedback by that Friday. This would allow the teachers to incorporate the feedback into their plans before actually teaching the lessons the next week. It was very time-consuming and demanding on both of us, but it was part of the model that we had formulated. We had to be dedicated to our part of the model if the teachers were going to be dedicated to their part.

Now that the planning requirements had been set and carefully explained, professional development turned from what to teach to *how* to teach. The delivery of instruction was the next step in the teaching and learning change process. The teachers' contract offered a template for lesson planning. My research also showed that the teachers would benefit from a template outlining how to effectively deliver a well-prepared lesson, a Lesson Delivery Model. Since I had nothing more concrete to go on to improve student outcomes, I decided to put the research to the test. The only effective model I ever saw used for teaching and learning was Madeline Hunter's seven-step lesson plan. My team and I took the seven-step framework and modified the components to include:

1. Review of Standard/Objective
2. Do Now
3. Teaching/Modeling

4. Guided Practice
5. Independent Practice
6. Small Group Instruction
7. Exit Ticket

Many teachers did not want to use a model, arguing that it was too much work. They made many calls to their union representative, and I received many calls from the teachers' union, but I was prepared for that. I referred each caller to a section of the teachers' contract that called for "Daily Activities including instructional strategies." The seven steps of the model became the instructional strategies. Framing the process around union language made the process contractual, but actually getting teachers to complete weekly lesson plans using the mandated, seven-step instructional strategies would prove to be one of the hardest things I ever had to do. But I had nothing else promising to get my children to learn. I had to stay the course.

All of the components of the seven-step plan were important for student learning, but small group instruction was the most important. Many of the students had difficulty following along during instruction. The teacher never moved on from an initial concept because many students were confused, leaving the advanced students in the class sitting idle. To complicate matters, many of the students were on different reading levels, and many had special needs and behavior challenges. Small group instruction would be our way to incorporate differentiation and give everyone the attention they needed. Here is where the students would receive individualized instruction to help fill in their educational gaps.

Getting high school teachers to comply with small group instruction (known as an elementary school intervention) would be difficult. They knew it was important, and they knew it would give the students what they needed to learn; however, once again, they believed it was too much work to plan an additional focus and conduct small groups within a 33-student class. Classroom management was always the concern. These were the two reasons cited for not wanting to use this strategy. To support them to this end, I hired Student Support Assistants who would be assigned to every math and English class during small group instruction. The teacher would work with a group of students, and the Student Support Assistant would monitor and answer questions for the students working independently. This would allow the teacher to stay focused on the students who needed the most help, without interruption.

The last step in the introduction of the teaching and learning system was the rollout of the informal and formal observations and feedback cycle. In order for all teachers to reflect on their teaching and learning practices, feedback would be crucial. A walkthrough protocol was developed to give instant feedback after every weekly informal observation. It was mandatory for administrators to provide each teacher with immediate feedback on the planning and delivery process. This feedback would be used to guide adjustments in the planning and delivery of instruction.

Regularly monitoring what goes on in the classroom is the only way to ensure that teachers are teaching what they said they would teach with fidelity. Many times school leaders fail to monitor and give regular feedback on the systems they have in place. Teachers are allowed to close their doors too often with no accountability. I know firsthand how dangerous that can be. Leaders must open their teachers' doors and have a seat in the classroom to ensure student learning. That was the goal of this entire system.

As our first day of professional development came to a close, many of the teachers looked overwhelmed. The teachers from Fitzsimons who had followed me to Rhodes were thrilled with anticipation. They knew the system was a lot of work, but that it was worth it. The teachers from Rhodes looked shocked at what I was asking, but I would not be swayed to do anything differently.

To wrap up our first day of professional development together, I showed the staff Michael Jackson's "Man in the Mirror" video. In it, he sings about how he will make the world a better place, starting with making changes in his own life and practices. I told the teachers that it was now up to us. The change begins with us. We know all of the challenges ahead, and we know what will happen if we fail. The last thing I asked them was to look in the mirror. There, they would see a lifesaver. I reminded them that it would be a lot of work; however, when we decided to become teachers, this is the work that we signed up for. Everyone filed out quietly—and hopefully, inspired.

## Thinking About Your Leadership

You must roll out your organization's system for change. Approaching others with a new way of doing things can be difficult. Many people would like to keep things the way they are, even if that way is not working. They like being comfortable. That is why the leader must be decisive in leading the change effort.

Try to think of every obstacle that can prevent you from succeeding, and address those obstacles before you meet with your staff. You do not want to introduce a plan if there is something in the company guidelines or union contract that can stop you cold in your tracks. Try to take away all of the excuses and have an answer to explain why things have to be different. Research your turnaround system. Find data that will support success in your situation. Finally, end your first professional development or staff meeting with something visual that aligns to your vision or your definition of what's at stake. You are trying to align your vision and their vision on your first encounter. Make it emotional! Inspire them.

**Examine Attentively:** The systematic approach needed to get your organization to immediately move in the right direction.

**Questions for You:**
- What is your system for turnaround?
- How will you inspire your team to forge ahead through challenging times?

# 7

# Unveil

On day two of teacher and support staff professional development prior to school opening—and before unveiling the final focus area to make Rhodes a great school—I showed a scene from the movie *Coach Carter*. I desperately needed to get them to understand that all of the extra effort needed to make our school successful would be worth it. I wanted to begin day two the way day one seemed to end: with being inspired!

When the young man said, "Coach, I just want to say thank you for saving my life," I stopped the tape. I turned to the teachers and gently said that if we worked together, saving lives would happen daily. I told them that a sincere "thank you" from a student would be their greatest reward for all of the hard work. "Thank you for saving my life!" I repeated it over and over, and looked at each staff member. "Ending the cycle of poverty," I reminded them. "That is the goal."

After recapping the expectations for teaching and learning, it was time to unveil the plan to address the third and final focus area for a successful school. The focus area that was of upmost importance to every member of the staff: school safety! Asking teachers to build meaningful relationships with the students and plan and deliver excellent lessons every day in a violent setting was an unreasonable request. Fear paralyzes even the best of us. There have been numerous occasions while I was a teacher when others used violence as a reason to lower student expectations.

That was not going to be the case at Rhodes. So how was my team going to create an environment in which relationships could be formed and teaching and learning could really happen? How were we going the ease the fear factor? I use the word "ease" because when you work in an urban school where crime is near the highest in the nation, there is always going to be some level of underlying fear. How were we going to keep these rival neighborhoods of young women from harming one another? How was the staff going to remain safe (something that did not happen in years past)? How were we going to get everyone unified around their roles in our quest to keep everyone safe? I strongly emphasized that concentrating on one of our three focus areas at a time was not going to help accomplish the goal of creating a great school to aid in ending student poverty. It would take working on all three focus areas simultaneously. I reminded everyone that building relationships, teaching and learning, and school safety all go hand in hand: If the entire school family built positive relationships with the students, and they received quality instruction in the classroom, then I truly believed that everyone would be safe.

All of the teachers, from both Fitzsimons and Rhodes, had similar stories to tell about constant fighting, hall walking, profanity, and noncompliance with every school rule. They all agreed that noncompliance with school rules led to the decay of their schools. After hearing all the horrible stories of assaults, destruction, and fear, I told the staff that the only way to make a school safe was to develop and strictly enforce a schoolwide discipline system. Everyone could not do her own thing. It had to be a well-thought-out system grounded in addressing the school's major problems and then communicated to all stakeholders.

The schoolwide discipline system centered around a clear set of rules, consequences, and rewards. After looking at the 2004–2005 school data report of the 132 serious incidents (which ranged from assaults on students and staff to weapons violations, drug violations, and sexual misconduct), the leadership team settled on five rules as the foundation for making Rhodes safe.

To make sure everyone clearly understood that the rules would be learned, followed, and monitored, I gave the rules a name: "Non-Negotiable." The Non-Negotiable rules were:

1. No fighting (physical or verbal), no profanity, and no bullying
2. No unauthorized exiting of the building, and no propping doors open
3. Uniform compliance at all times
4. No cell phones
5. No inciting riots, or bringing in weapons or drugs

To ensure that the students were in compliance with the rules at all times, consequences for noncompliance with them were outlined. The leadership team decided that there would be six possible consequences for noncompliance with the school rules:

1. Phone call to parent
2. Detention
3. Parent conference
4. In-school suspension
5. Out-of-school suspension
6. Exclusion from activity

As a side note, all of these consequences are not uncommon. What would be uncommon for the entire school community would be our relentless system for ensuring compliance with the non-negotiable school rules. When the rules were not followed, an appropriate consequence would immediately be given to the student, then tracked and recorded for compliance. If the student did not comply with the consequence for his or her actions, an additional consequence would be given, mandating that a parent, guardian, or any other person designated by the parent visit the school for an in-depth conversation about the child's refusal to comply with school rules.

The Non-Negotiable Schoolwide Discipline System would also include rewards. We wanted rewards to replace consequences. It would be a sure sign that school was starting to feel like a safe place. Besides, positive relationships form when students and school staff interact and do fun things together. It gives the students time to talk, and gives the adults time to listen. Participation in all activities, clubs, and recognition ceremonies would hinge upon adhering to the school's Non-Negotiable Schoolwide Discipline System. Here are a few of the rewards the team came up with:

1. Field Day
2. No Uniform Day
3. Overnight Camping Retreats
4. College Trips
5. Field Trips—everywhere from the zoo to Washington D.C., to Baltimore Harbor, to New York City
6. Mural Painting
7. Assembly Programs
8. Career Day
9. Valentine Dance
10. Sophomore Hop
11. Reward Presentations

Just to name a few. More would be added with student input. We wanted to have so many activities planned for them that they would want to be present and allowed to participate. School was supposed to be fun. We wanted them to take part in activities they had never been exposed to before. However, it would be up to us as a school family to make sure the students were clear that the rules had to be followed in order for any participation. Our position was non-negotiable!

Day three of professional development was devoted to class-room preparation. The teachers were informed that every room would be inspected prior to school opening. Teachers were directed to decorate every bulletin board with motivational sayings or content-specific information. The way a classroom looks when a student enters it tells you a lot about the teacher. I wanted my teachers to make a good impression on their students from day one. Historically, the high school teachers were not like elementary teachers when it came to room decorations, but that all had to change at Rhodes. If it was not their best work, they would be asked to redo it prior to student arrival. While the teachers were busy beautifying their classrooms, the leadership team had the responsibility of beautifying the entire school. Every single bulletin board outside of the classrooms was completed by the leadership team.

After three days of professional development, the first day of school was fast approaching. We had prepared as a newly formed staff. It was now time to put the entire plan into motion: build positive relationships among the students and staff so that school could be fun; implement a teaching and learning system that would yield results; and prove that with clear behavioral expectations, even schools considered notoriously violent can be made safe for everyone. I ended professional development by trying to inspire the teachers and support staff once more. I told them that, when the work gets to be too much to bear, to pretend that the students who sit before them are their own children and push a little harder. Want for someone else's child what you would want for your own. Then I turned on a clip from the ending of the movie *To Sir, with Love.*

The song and the images of the students saying "thank you" and "so long" to their teacher made everyone feel proud to be a teacher. We left the room together prepared to open the Young Women's Leadership School at Rhodes for the first time.

The young women filed into the classrooms looking absolutely beautiful in their yellow and gray uniforms on the first day of school. They went directly to advisory without incident. We were off to a great start, even though, after much prompting from community leaders, we had decided to hire many young men from the neighborhood to patrol the line that the young women from Fitzsimons had to cross to get to Rhodes. The time came for all the students and staff to report to the auditorium to review our plan for a successful school opening and year. It was my job as principal to present the focus areas to the students. I talked about the fun we would have working together. I discussed my teaching and learning expectations of the staff and the students. Then I presented the Non-Negotiable Schoolwide Discipline System for the first time to the students (and once more for the staff). I wanted everyone in the school to hear the plan together so there would be no confusion. I projected the schoolwide behavior system as I carefully explained each rule, consequence, and reward. I repeatedly stressed how closely it would be monitored. To make sure that every student and every staff member was on the same page and very clear about the system, I held the same assembly program each of the first five days of school. I never wanted to hear anyone saying she did not know about a particular rule, consequence, or our desire to make school fun. The students were tired of hearing about the system, but they could not say they did not know it.

After the fifth day of the schoolwide behavior system presentation, I had every student sign for a handbook in advisory. In that handbook was a written version of the system for the students and their parents. Their signatures were an acknowledgment that the system had been explained to them, and that a written version had been given to them to give to their parents.

From the first day to the last day of school, the schoolwide behavior system was monitored every day by a team of people who had exceptional organizational skills. Of course it was Ms. Jackson who held everyone accountable for every part of the system, because, as I explained earlier, organization was a skill she was born with. At every leadership team meeting, we talked about the non-negotiables, but the five rules we started with never had to be adapted. We were on target with the right rules.

During the 2005–2006 school year, the serious incidents at The Young Women's Leadership School at Rhodes dropped from 132 to 20. A schoolwide discipline system was needed in order to make Rhodes a school. Students should know the behaviors that are expected of them. High school should mirror the real world. You get rewarded for excellence and a consequence for noncompliance with the law. This is how we keep young women out of the school-to-prison pipeline. We teach them the system while they are still in school.

After the opening days of school, we were back in professional development. This time, I ended the session by showing a clip from the movie *Drumline* where the band leader asks, "What is our concept?" All of the band members say, "One beat, one sound." The staff were no longer sitting on opposite sides of the room. Because of our carefully thought-out plan for building relationships, teaching and learning, and school safety, we finally started to function as one school community! One beat, one sound.

## Thinking About Your Leadership

Clear communication of the system for turnaround is key. You will need everyone to clearly understand the plan and why the components of the plan are the focus. You, the leader, should take the time to explain everything thoroughly. The entire turnaround team must understand that some strategies will be non-negotiable because the leadership team has completed the research and is confident of the strategy. Once a system is unveiled, a system for monitoring and adapting must be maintained.

**Examine Attentively:** The non-negotiables for your organization's success.

**Questions for You:**
- How will you unveil your system for change to all stakeholders?
- What are the "non-negotiables" that will lead to positive outcomes for your organization?

# 8

# Implement

All of the areas needed to make Rhodes a school had been addressed, and implementation of the system for change was well underway. We encountered many challenges in keeping with our "one beat, one sound" motto well into the school year. The old Fitzsimons staff believed in the systems, but the staff from Rhodes complained continually about the workload and often stated that the expectations were unrealistic.

The implementation of the teaching and learning system proved to be the most challenging for the teachers. To help keep the teachers continuously trying to improve in that area, the leadership team decided to get the students involved in the teaching and learning process. The students started to hold the teachers accountable for following the daily instructional model. They emphasized to their teachers the importance of conducting small group instruction even when they did not want to do it. They explained to their teachers that they enjoyed getting the help they needed during the class period, because many were unable to stay after school for tutoring. Even though it was a welcome addition by the students and we were gratified with the way they were taking charge of their own learning, the teachers were relentless in their complaints about the amount of planning it took to run an effective small group. Nonetheless, because it was non-negotiable, they forged ahead. By the end of our first year at Rhodes, we managed to raise the test scores in math and English, but fell just short of the Adequate Yearly Progress (AYP) target set by the state of Pennsylvania. We celebrated our growth, but AYP was the goal we were aiming for.

While many of the teachers and staff thought that our missing the goal slightly was some kind of conspiracy, I used that energy to get everyone even more focused and motivated. We had a great teaching and learning system in place, and the instructional model was everything the research said it would be, but something was still missing. The leadership team and I went in search of the answer.

We opened the 2006–2007 school year determined to make our AYP target. We spent the entire summer reviewing the data to figure out what our teaching and learning system was missing. One day during our leadership team meeting, we received a visit from our EMO superintendent. He walked in, and said:

> You have a great teaching and learning system. You concentrate on curriculum, preparation and planning, and delivery of instruction. You have the buy-in from the students. You have the observations and the feedback. But what you are missing is a relentless focus on the student mastery data. Have you drilled down your focus to note which skills the students have mastered and which ones they have not? Yes, the scores increased, but which skills did they master and which ones do they still have to master based on state data, not teacher data? Do you know that? Are the teachers planning their small groups with that in mind? Are the teachers grouping them according to their areas of need?

Even though I used data to make a lot of decisions, I had to admit I did not use the data in the way he had described. We had tried everything else. This had to be the missing variable. Small group instruction became even more important. It was our remediation and our acceleration plan for each student, our time to work with the individual students on what they did not know and understand.

We asked the teachers to look at the data and group the students according to their challenge areas, or the areas in which they could be advanced. During small group instruction, the focus became that particular content. Data collection for each standard was mandatory. Throughout the process, the teachers once again complained about the workload, and once again, I explained that teaching children what they need to know is not too much for a teacher to handle. Many of them did not agree with me, but more were getting on board as they witnessed their students learning.

We grew relentless in the individual review of student data. We knew every skill that every student knew and did not know. We gave additional homework according to where they needed support with eligible content. The Pennsylvania Department of Education defines "eligible content" as the most specific description of the skills and concepts assessed on the state assessment. This level is considered the assessment limit, and helps educators identify the range of the content covered on the exam.

After the first benchmark exam, and after research suggested that we provide more time on task as a strategy to improve student learning, the leadership team felt compelled to add one more component to the teaching and learning system: "more time on task."

This one was difficult. Staying after school for our students was not possible. Many of them were mothers, they worked, or they took care of a family member. We understood that, so we had to remediate them further during the school day. So we turned to the master schedule to find the time. The only place in the schedule where we could find more time to remediate the students was the lunch period. It was 50 minutes long. We started to question, "Did the students need 50 minutes to eat lunch?" We decided the answer was "No." So we designed a program called "Lunch and More." The students ate lunch for 30 minutes and were tutored or counseled for the other 20 minutes. The students who needed help with academics were tutored on the data-directed skills, and students who were lacking confidence had counseling sessions with the counselor. "Lunch and More" allowed us to provide more time on task in academic areas, and addressed many needed social and emotional issues in the process.

At the time that all of this was happening in the school, I was having some deeply personal challenges. My mother was very ill. She had diabetes, with a lot of complications. Over the years she always bounced back. This time was different. After school was over each day, I would go to the hospital to spend time with her and have deeply personal conversations. My mother was my rock. She was my hero. She had made it her business in life to always take care of her three children. Education for my mother was everything. Being poor should make you value education, she would say. She always believed it was our way out of poverty. That is why every bus ride was a time to teach us about what we could have in life. Her health was getting worse. When I would visit her, I would ask her if she wanted me to take a leave of absence to sit with her. She would always tell me no! She would say, "Those children need you and I taught you that if you have a job, you go to work." Even though we were poor, we were among the working poor. My mother always had a job, and always went to work.

I would go back and forth, from the school to the hospital. It was my way of life that year. She was not getting better. While I was dealing with the imminent death of my mother, I was still trying to get the school to move further in the right direction. My staff and I had worked so hard to make Adequate Yearly Progress. We wanted to prove to everyone that our children in the 19132 zip code could learn just like everyone else if they had focused teachers and a person to lead them.

While visiting my mother in the hospital one day, she whispered that she was tired of fighting. They wanted her to have one more surgery, but she had refused. My sisters called me in a last-ditch effort to persuade her to have the surgery and prolong her life a little longer. My mother and I were very close. I always found myself being her protector. I was the assertive person she could never be. She was always soft-spoken, and I was always outspoken. Together, we made a team. I told my mother this would be the last time I would ask her to fight, but that I needed her to fight this time. She agreed to have the surgery.

While waiting for the surgery to take place, thoughts of the students and the staff weighed heavily on my mind. But state testing was weeks away, and I knew we had done everything we could to prepare. All we could do now was to continue the systems until testing day.

My mother did not do well after the surgery. She was told that she could not go home and would have to go to a nursing facility. She repeatedly told me that she was not going to a nursing facility; she was going home. On the day my mother was supposed to be transported to a nursing facility, she was sent back to the ICU. The doctor told my sisters and me that we had to make a decision. How long were we going to keep her hooked up to the machines in pain, just to keep her alive because we could not let go? We decided that she was in too much pain, and we promised her after the last surgery that we would not ask for her to fight anymore. She was our mother, so we had to keep our promise. We could not continue to make her suffer. She had been a mother that anyone would dream of having, but she belonged to God. The machines went away, and we prepared for God to take her home, where she wanted to be. We did not want her to die alone, so we took turns staying with her every minute. My shift was after school each day. It was funny, but I knew that my mother would not die on my shift. We had spent too many great times together; and she knew she was my life, and that I would do anything to keep her with me.

I was right. She did not die on my shift, or on my younger sister Denise's shift. Denise was her baby, and she always protected her from pain. She went to God with my sister Andrea by her side at 6:00 a.m. Andrea was the oldest. Mom always did do things in the proper order. When I received the call from my sister, I thought the world would stop. I remember looking at the clock the minute my sister called me and said she was dead. Then I looked at the clock a minute later. I thought it could not be so, but time was still moving.

I buried my mother a few weeks before the state test. I was determined to lead the school to reaching our goal, even though I was having my own personal challenges. I felt good when the week of testing finally came, because I knew I had done everything I could to honor, protect, obey, and deliver on my promise to my mother to give her a fulfilled, stress-free life once I educated myself. And because I knew I had done everything I could think of in order for my students to be successful.

We made Adequate Yearly Progress in 2007, our second year at Rhodes. In that same year, the girl who had told me her school was "not a school" graduated from high school. We had made the school a school. I was so glad she was around to witness what a real school can do: find academic success, build character, teach self-discipline, expose students to the world, and then send them out into that world. She not only graduated from high school, but she went to college. She was among our first graduating class, which had a 95 percent college acceptance rate.

My mother would have been so proud. We often talked about the goals I had for my students. It felt good leading children to success on the test, but we still had much more to do. In order to make the school a school, it was our goal to help every child become proficient on the state examination.

In 2008, we missed our AYP graduation rate target. That was a measurement that the school had no control over, because of our enormous transient population. Students who started with us in ninth grade moved several times in their high school years, but they still counted for the first high school they entered as a freshman. However, we met all of our academic targets.

The year 2009, however, brought our biggest test to date. For some reason that year, we had a lot of new teachers who felt that the system was too much work. So over the course of the school year, and eight weeks before the state assessment, every English teacher quit. We were faced with no English teachers to teach the students eight weeks before state testing. We were in a bind. The leadership team and I knew we had to figure it out, but together, we could not come up with any solution for replacing the English teachers. Substitute teachers would only want to babysit the students. They would never be able to institute the systems we had in place. What were we going to do without English teachers? I could not get this dilemma off of my mind. I would sit in my blue leadership chair and think about it all day, and I had a lot of sleepless nights. I was the school leader and it was my job to come up with the answer, even if the team could not.

How could I replace three English teachers at one time? I started to total up the students from all three classes who needed to be tested. It was nearly 99 students. I asked myself, how could I teach so many levels at one time? Then, I thought about the library. It was a beautiful space. We had replaced all of the broken furniture, and we had many desktop computers there. There it was. I devised a plan that I would teach all 99 students myself in the library. I needed the help of two people: Ms. Jackson and a noontime aide. Ms. Jackson would make sure the library was fully equipped with the resources I needed, and the noontime aide would help me with the paperwork. It was her responsibility to grade all of the assignments. I also needed help with what I would teach them. Then I thought about small groups, and the focus on individual students' skill development. I found a computer program that focused on every assessment anchor and eligible content that would be tested on the state exam, and it aligned with the curriculum from the district. I was ready to start teaching my 99 students.

Every day, the classes were escorted to the library, where the noontime aide and I would assign students to every computer. Students who did not have a computer sat with me for small group instruction. The students and the staff thought I was crazy. The teachers and other staff members would walk into the library on their prep period and just stare at the students working alone with me. I knew some of them thought, "That is what she gets for making us work so hard," but others became even more invested.

One day, as I was working with the students, a teacher came though on her preparation period. Instead of staring at me, she asked, "Mrs. Wayman, what can I do to help you?" What she did not know was that it was week two of me going solo, and I was getting tired—but I had to make it work. I had to let the teachers and staff understand that I was the leader and I was not going to let 99 children sit with no teacher for eight weeks, then be asked to take a state exam. I was prepared to forge ahead. I looked at the data and told her that one group of girls still needed help with this particular skill. She sat down and tutored those girls on her preparation period. She did not ask me for compensation. She just helped the students. That started an enormous amount of support. All of the teachers who believed in our ability to teach these students through difficult times joined me on their prep periods to help the students learn. We started to hand out prizes to keep the students motivated to do well, and we had turned a horrible situation into a relationship-building exercise.

Even with all the staff support, the school family could not overcome this huge obstacle of filling the void of three English teachers without some additional outside assistance. We formed a wonderful service-learning partnership with Villanova University, whose students would come from the Main Line to North Philadelphia twice a week to help tutor my students in English or math. The partnership was invaluable. The students were so patient, kind, and helpful. Every time they walked into the library prepared to help my students, I really wanted to cry. I needed their help, and they were willing to help. Most people will remember Villanova University for their nationally ranked basketball team, but my students and staff will remember them as the school that cared enough to make sure children they barely knew had a chance at life.

I taught in the library until it was time for state testing. I missed a lot of deadlines and I was late for many meetings. When I had to attend a meeting, I taught others how to run the process for me. The show had to go on, whether I was there or not.

The day before we took the state exam in 2009, the leadership team held an assembly program. We call it the "PUSH" assembly. We wanted to tell the students how special they were. We told them we were proud of their efforts. We reminded them that they were smart, intelligent, and prepared for the assessment, and we told them what we expected from them. I then decided to give them a history lesson. Since my students were 100 percent African American, I had one of my history teachers put together a PowerPoint of African American history highlighting the many sacrifices made by African Americans in order for them to be able to dream. I showed them examples of times in history when others were asked to push through their circumstances to excel in difficult times, and they did. I told them that it was now their time to show that they were indeed educated and on the path to make a difference in the next era of American history. At the end of that assembly, we told them how much we loved them—*very* much.

In 2009, we made Adequate Yearly Progress again. Everyone was overjoyed! We had worked together as a team to accomplish our goal. But our students deserve the recognition. They pushed through all of their fears and feelings about being tested, and focused on making themselves and their school proud. This was the work we were most proud of, because we did it together unselfishly.

In 2010, we met all of our academic targets, but missed AYP on something that the school had no control over. It was a district problem related to how they calculated graduation rate. It was clear that our teaching and learning focus was correct, and our climate system was perfect. The serious incidents in 2010 fell to just five. Over the course of five years, we had moved the proficiency rate from 3 percent in math and 9 percent in English to nearly 50 percent in math and over 50 percent in English. We had made Rhodes a school. We were proud of our students, our staff, our system, and most of all, our ability to implement it at all costs. I was proud that we had figured it all out. All students can learn, but schools need leaders to put systems in place for them do so.

During our last professional development in June 2010, I thanked my staff for helping students who live in poverty see that whatever they put their minds to is possible. I thanked the teachers and the support staff for helping our school defy the odds. I also told them that we had to be careful, because we knew the secret to success. And I predicted that one day, they would close the school we had created—a school for young women who live in a poverty-stricken neighborhood that did not select children, and was able to pass the state exam. They looked at me in shock and asked, "Why would they do that?" I told them, "I do not have the answer to that question, but they will find a way to close the school; remember, I told you that."

To end the professional development session for that year, I showed them a clip of the song "We Haven't Finished Yet" from the movie *The Five Heartbeats*. "No matter how hard it gets, we haven't finished yet," sang the chorus.

Little did I know at the time that would be my final professional development with the staff at Rhodes. Due to the success of my second merger and my ability to lead my staff in academic outcomes for students, I was asked to be the Assistant Superintendent for High Schools for Philadelphia during the summer of 2010.

## Thinking About Your Leadership

Sometimes the plan for success falls short from the goal. The best thing to do is to review the plan over and over to see what is missing. Sometimes it will take an objective eye. Consult with others outside of the team, and welcome a new point of view. When you've figured out what is missing from the action plan, find a way to infuse it into the existing program. There is no need to scrap all the parts of the plan. Just find where the new part fits and move forward.

Know that unexpected things will happen in your personal life and within the plan. Leaders find ways to handle both situations. True leaders lead when everything seems hopeless. LEAD!

**Examine Attentively:** Your mindset around leadership. Sometimes you will have to make all the sacrifices to make the mission a success.

**Questions for You:**
- How do you handle personal and professional responsibilities in your leadership role?
- Are you willing to do what needs to be done yourself to make sure the mission is successful?

## 9

# Amplify

I packed up all my belongings and walked out of the Young Women's Leadership School at Rhodes in the middle of July 2010 after returning from a meeting with the superintendent. Leaving Rhodes was the hardest thing I had ever done professionally. I loved what we had created by staying true to the goals of cultivating positive relationships among the school family, teaching and learning, and safety. Merging two schools into one had been very hard, but we did it successfully and created a school that the community could be proud of.

The day I departed, I decided that Ms. Jackson would be the only person present to assist me. She had been with me from the start of this journey until this moment. I did not want anyone else to see me cry as hard as I did. Through my tears, I thought about what had happened in the superintendent's office, and I knew that it was time for me to leave.

When the superintendent summoned me to her office while I was still on vacation, I knew it was important, but I had no idea what the meeting would be about. When I got to her office, she immediately started interviewing me for a job for which I did not apply, and asked me if I would consider accepting the position of Assistant Superintendent for High Schools. I knew about the posting, but had never considered applying for it. I loved Rhodes and had no plans to leave. After she reviewed the requirements for the job, I thanked her for the offer. Then

I said, "No thank you, I cannot leave my school." It shocked me when she said, "Your school? Rhodes is not your school." That was the first time I had ever heard anyone say that Rhodes was not my school. I was the founding principal of the Young Women's Leadership School at Rhodes. Of course it was my school. She continued, "If I wanted to, I could move you tomorrow to another school." The sound of that made me panic inside. "Move me?" My heart started racing. "As superintendent," she said, "I can move you to any school I choose."

I must have looked so frightened that she calmed down and said, "Look, Mrs. Wayman, everyone in the district that I talk to about you says you have courage. I need someone who has courage to lead the high schools and to coach the leaders to be more effective. They also say you are not afraid to tell people what you have to tell them." As she talked, I began to calm down and listen more intently. "I need you to take the job, because that is what it will take to lead children out of poverty: a person who has courage. Also, in order for you to really help the children in need you are going to have to see this from the inside." There was something about that statement that I could not get out of my mind: You have to see it from the inside if you are going to continue to help children in need.

The superintendent gave me a 24-hour deadline to give her an answer, and I accepted the position. I needed to see it from the inside. I needed to be inside the superintendent's office to understand the rationale for the decisions that were affecting my students. I had to take this opportunity and see it for myself, and change what I could change for the good of the children.

The last item that I packed in my car was my blue leadership chair. I sat in it until it was time for me to walk out the door and remembered all of the decisions that I had made while sitting in the chair. I thought about the journey from Fitzsimons to Rhodes, and all we had accomplished with a student setting the vision for us. I placed the chair in my van and drove away crying uncontrollably.

I was now the leader of 52 high schools, and it was my main job to get the leaders to own the outcomes of their own leadership. The year 2010 was a tough time to begin my career as an assistant superintendent. There were plans underway to close, consolidate, or turn schools over to charter schools across the district as part of the new Facilities Master Plan. I was new to central office, so I did a lot of observing. At first I enjoyed nothing about working out of central office, and I was often annoyed by the lack of times I heard the word "children." Even though I was new, in most meetings I was one of few people who reminded everyone why we were there: for the children. Politics was always front and center. The conversations were mainly about what could not be done, rather than what could be done. Everything was an excuse for why something could not happen, and no one wanted to make a final decision for anything. I could not understand that, and I grew more and more frustrated each day. I was not the only person who was frustrated. The students in many of the schools being considered for closure, consolation, or charter were also frustrated. Getting definitive answers was difficult, leaving everyone involved annoyed.

Working with the school leaders was the important work of my job. Trying to get all the principals to lead with confidence and skill forced me to model both of those things often. The principals who were leading the schools through these difficult times needed more support than ever.

One day I received a phone call informing me that the students at Martin Luther King High School were expected to walk out at 12:00 p.m. because they did not want to become a charter school. My directive was to get over there and prevent the students from walking out en masse. I was also told that a lot of support would be there to help me stop the students from walking out of school. When I walked into the school, I met with my support team sent from the superintendent's office, a male community member and a representative from the charter organization set to acquire the school. The principal of the school and his assistant principals were also present. We sat around the table trying to come up with a blueprint for how we were going to avoid the walkout. The principal was an interim principal who needed a lot of support to help him though this difficult situation. As we sat around the table trying to come up with a plan, the building felt toxic. It felt like it was going to erupt into a mass of destruction. Tempers were flaring. I asked the principal to tell me about what was happening in the building. Why were the students and staff so angry? The principal said it was all related to the charter takeover and who had the right to the charter. While he was speaking, I was watching the clock. All I could think of was my directive: "the students better not walk out of school." My support team had no answers. As time went on, I knew that if something positive was going to happen, I would have to take the lead. I am one person, I remember thinking: How could I possibly stop nearly 800 students from walking out of school?

If I was the principal, then I could have stopped them from walking out easily because of the relationship I had with my students. So I took my assistant superintendent hat off and stepped into the role of principal. One of my strengths was my ability to relate to young adults. I stopped focusing on the adults, and focused on the children. The one thing I knew for sure was that young adults between the ages of 14 to 20 liked to be heard. I told the principals and the assistant principals to send me all of the leaders in the school. I was not just talking about the honor students or the students on the debate team. I was talking about the students other students would say ran the school. The students who liked to walk the halls, the students who liked to cause problems, the students who were known in their neighborhoods as tough guys, the students suspended most frequently. I asked them to bring me all of these students and meet me in the library. There ended up being about 60 to 70 students, and they were ready for a fight. They came in with their signs, screaming and hollering, "Walkout, walkout!" I stood up, looked them in the eye, and in a firm but sympathetic voice asked, "Walkout for what?"

"Before we get started with the answers to that question, we will have to set some ground rules," I announced. "I have to listen to you attentively without interruption, and when you ask me a question you have to listen to me without interruption." Then I waved my arm in the air and said, "Go ahead now—one at a time—and tell me what is going on!" They proceeded to tell me everything they saw wrong with the process for their school to become a charter school. "We do not want to be a charter school." "We do not want to wear uniforms." "We do not want to lose our teachers." I told them to keep talking and keep asking me questions. Some of them were very rude, and some were pleasant. I listened to all of them. I listened and talked with the student leaders until 11:50 a.m. The walkout was set for noon. I talked so much that when my supervisor walked into the room I had no voice left. When I opened my mouth, you could barely hear a sound come out.

I ended our conversation by telling them that they were heard, and that something would be done. I promised them that in the most sincere voice I had left. Then I glanced at the time ticking away on the clock. "Right now I am asking you to please call off the student walkout," I continued. "You prepared the walkout for someone to listen. I listened. This school is a school under my leadership, and I promised you something would be done." Then I reminded them that something had already been done. Someone had listened. There was a moment of silence from the entire library full of people. Then it was announced over the public address system that "There will be no walkout."

For the next minute I held my breath and prayed to God that nearly 800 students would not walk out of that building. The news cameras were waiting in position. But the walkout never happened. The newspaper reported that around 70 students had walked out. That was not the truth. The students who had walked out at noon had work rosters, and were leaving at their normal time. A few of them were holding signs, but those were the signs they had prepared to walk out with.

That was one of the first incidents when I had to demonstrate for one of my leaders how to lead. Think outside the box, put it all on the line, and pray that you are skilled enough to be triumphant in the end. Remember what you do well, and use that in various situations. Sometimes, you just have to go for it. That is what I wanted to demonstrate for my principals. Try your best! I still hope that I modeled confidence and skill that day. Martin Luther King High School never became a charter school, by the way—the students really did win in the end.

As assistant superintendent, I enjoyed leading the principals the most. Amplifying my skills to help leaders help children was a great experience. I was able to get to know each high school intimately, and to observe the uniqueness of every individual principal and each of their school families.

Leaving Rhodes was difficult. However, the superintendent was correct. Seeing how a school district operates from the inside is very eye-opening, and oftentimes frightening. You begin to understand why conditions for students are challenging. Central office and schools must incorporate the "one beat, one sound" motto if all children are going to succeed. As Assistant Superintendent for High Schools, I had the opportunity to learn and experience things that would prove valuable in the future. Yet at the time, it made me wonder, "Why me?" Why did the superintendent choose me to see it all?

## Thinking About Your Leadership

Once turnaround happens and the organization has a focus and a vision, it may be time for you to seek new and challenging opportunities. Leaving something you help to create and build can be difficult. When opportunities arise, think about why the opportunity may be a time to experience growth. The only way to grow as a leader is to stretch into new leadership roles. That can be overwhelming, but necessary. People will come into your life and force you to see things you do not see. These people are there to lead you further on your journey, and they will be witnesses to your transformation as a leader.

**Examine Attentively:** When it is time to take an expanded leadership role.

**Questions for You:**

- Do you recognize the signs that it is time for you to amplify and expand your leadership influence?

- What situations caused you to draw upon skills others may not have known you had?

# 10

# Prepare

During my second year as Assistant Superintendent for High Schools, the Facility Master Plan continued to control my work. School closures, consolidations, relocations, and charters were the daily talk of conversation at central office and in the community. No one wanted to close schools, and no one wanted their school to close, but the districts kept their position that the underutilization of buildings was costing large sums of money that the district simply could not afford. It was just a mess. A way to cut operational costs had to be found, but none of the schools affected wanted to hear about cutting costs when it impacted their school. The community meetings were brutal. The yelling, the screaming, and the threats aimed at me as I tried to explain to school communities that had been around for many years that their school had to close took a toll on me night after night.

The ironic thing was that I found myself facilitating the community meetings about the possible closure of my own high school. It felt strange standing there in the front of the auditorium, looking out at a handful of people who were trying to make their point for why this school should stay open or should close. While standing there as assistant superintendent, I could only think about sitting in the same auditorium in 1976, witnessing all the chaos and regretting not listening to my mother when she suggested that I go to another school. I thought about the poor

67

education I had received at that school and my decision to go to college. I felt sad standing there, but thought about how life had finally come full circle. This school had a long history with plenty of important alumni, but only a handful of people came out to save the school from a charter takeover. We had a lot of security that night because we thought this community meeting was going to be the worst one so far, but it was uneventful. I realized as I listened that the school meant nothing to me, and the small turnout showed that it was not a major priority for others either. At the end of the meeting, I felt a sense of closure. The school would be taken over by a charter, and that was that. I realized that my experience here in this school helped shape my purpose in life: saving poor children through education. I suddenly let all of my anger go and realized that it was all supposed to happen this way.

During the 2011–2012 school year, the School Reform Commission (school board) and the superintendent's office were under increased pressure to make more decisions about closing schools per the Facility Master Plan recommendations. There were many schools on the list; among them was the Young Men's Leadership School at Fitzsimons. It made the list because its enrollment was below 400 students and the building had the capacity to hold more than 1,000 students. Also included on the list was the Young Women's Leadership School at Rhodes. Rhodes had approximately 400 students, and the building capacity was near 1,200. There were many reasons for low enrollment in both schools. Many parents did not like gender-separate schools, and the reputation of both schools was still poor, even after major changes. Also, school choice gave the students many options they did not have in the past, and charters in that community were developing rapidly.

After a long-fought battle from students, teachers, unions, community groups, and parents, the decision was made to close The Young Men's Leadership School at Fitzsimons and relocate the Young Women's Leadership School at Rhodes to another building, making the Rhodes building a K-8 school. The superintendent felt that the Rhodes building could serve a larger population of students if it was a K-8 school, thus using more of the building space.

Watching these decisions unfold was heartbreaking. I argued behind closed doors for why Rhodes should not relocate. Fitzsimons had more pressing problems than space, so I knew I was not going to win that argument, even though Fitzsimons had come a long way since the day I took over. I felt so torn between my loyalty to the central office team and my love for a school I had started. All of the hard work that went into creating those two schools less than 10 years earlier was now headed down the drain. I recalled my last conversation with my staff at Rhodes. I told them that one day they would find a way to close Rhodes. They asked me, "How would they close it? We have made academic progress each year." I told them that I did not know how they were going to do it, but they would find a way. In my heart I knew it. It turned out that my instincts were correct—and ironically, I was part of the team that closed it.

When it was announced that Fitzsimons would close and Rhodes would relocate, my phone rang off the hook that evening from my former staff members who had attended that final meeting. They were calling to see whether I recalled my last conversation with them.

They did not call it a closure, because Rhodes the school did not close. It went back to its original school name, E. W. Rhodes Middle School. But the school as it was in my time as principal no longer existed. They left the seventh- and eighth-graders and sent over the Kindergarten through sixth-grade students from other schools. Students in grades nine to twelve were relocated elsewhere. The students from both Fitzsimons and Rhodes would merge into a school called Strawberry Mansion High School.

Strawberry Mansion High School was selected because it has a building capacity for over 1,600 students. At that time, it was housing fewer than 400 students. The school was also newly renovated. It had state-of-the-art science labs, a brand-new culinary facility, and a beautiful new library. The construction of the building was ideal for a state-of-the-art school. The possibility of what the school could become was the focus. However, Strawberry Mansion High School had many internal problems. Principal turnovers, violent assaults on students and staff, arrests, and weapon violations forced them to be on the nation's Persistently Dangerous Schools list for five consecutive years. In addition, Strawberry Mansion, Fitzsimons, and Rhodes had a long history of rivalry. They all were situated in North Philadelphia in the 39th and 22nd police districts, where crime is rampant. Leading Strawberry Mansion before the merger was problematic for my team. Successfully leading a two-school merger into Strawberry Mansion would take a lot of planning.

During the community hearings, the students and parents of the Fitzsimons and Rhodes Schools were promised that they would not be forced into Strawberry Mansion High School. They were told that if they met the academic requirements for any other school, they would be given first choice to attend that school in the high school selection process. This news excited the parents from Rhodes and Fitzsimons. They saw this as an opportunity to place their children in a school better than the one they were coming from and to avoid being sent to Strawberry Mansion.

I turned my attention from the depression of the school closure and relocation to explaining to the parents that this could be a great opportunity to get their child into a "high quality seat" (the term we used when students moved from a low-performing school to a higher-performing school). I felt good about the idea of this happening. I personally talked with many of the parents from Rhodes and Fitzsimons and explained the process of selecting a school to them. If I could not keep the schools open, I could at least make sure that the children got into a school of their choice.

I facilitated the entire process. I asked each of the current principals to develop a process for determining where the students wanted to attend high school. The principal provided me with the students' choices, and I submitted them to Student Placement. Representatives from Student Placement and I consulted on many occasions on where the young men and young women would attend high school, but we kept running into problems getting many of the students admitted to schools of their choice. A few principals had expressed that they did not want to take the students from Fitzsimons and Rhodes, even though they were qualified or barely missed an entrance requirement, such as one additional instance of tardiness over the limit. I was so frustrated that I wanted to force the principals to take the students, but I was advised against that tactic.

So that left one choice for the majority of students from Rhodes and Fitzsimons. They would be assigned to Strawberry Mansion High School.

I did not receive many calls from the students or parents of the young men, so the majority of them stayed on the list to attend Strawberry Mansion. The young women were a different story. The young women sent many emails questioning their new location. I had assured them that they would end up in a school suited for them. In my heart they were still my students, and I was still their principal. I had this sense of responsibility toward them that I could not get rid of. I talked to many parents who were sad about the young women having to leave Rhodes, and upset with me as assistant superintendent for not saving the high school from relocation. I went to work every day with a heavy heart. Who would take care of my students? My seventh-graders while I was principal at Rhodes were now in the tenth grade. I knew all of them personally.

There was one student in particular. She was an honor student and worked very hard in school. She was kind, a leader, smart, respectful of adults, and college bound. She was the kind of student everyone adored. She was always special to me. I had to make sure she was in the right school.

I got the word while sitting in my blue leadership chair at the office one day that she was not going to the school I thought I had secured for her. I was devastated. It turns out that she and other students were told their school placements for the 2012 school year by the school counselor on the last day of school in June. The counselor relayed this information to the students based on the information she had received from Student Placement with my signoff. Everyone left for the summer believing they were going somewhere other than Strawberry Mansion, even though they had nothing in writing. In August, my honor student received a letter from Student Placement that said she was assigned to Strawberry Mansion, not the special admit school she was promised. Her father called Student Placement and was told that since some of the young women on the list did not meet the entrance requirement, the principal decided not to admit any of them. I felt like I had failed her and her father. I felt terrible. I knew firsthand what she would be walking into at Strawberry Mansion if the problems there were not rectified.

As leader of the high schools, I knew the first thing that I had to do to make sure all of the students were safe and educated was to find a principal who could handle a three-way high school merger, believed to be the first of its kind in Philadelphia. If I could not prevent the merger or get the students into better schools, I had to make sure the merger was successful. The only way of giving this merger a chance at success was to hire a competent school leader, but after the national search, I had no candidates for the job. I lost a lot of sleep worrying about the students' safety if a competent school leader could not be found. I began to look internally. I made a list of all 52 principals under my leadership. My team and I critiqued each one of them, carefully looking at strengths and weaknesses. Those critique sessions only yielded one candidate out of the 52.

If you remember the Introduction of this book, you know what happened next.

I realized that I was supposed to go Strawberry Mansion. I was the only one really prepared to go. I had been through two other mergers, as no other principal in Philadelphia had. I knew what the students would face when they went into Strawberry Mansion, because Strawberry Mansion was presently under my leadership. They would not notice the physical renovations, because the emotional conditions would devastate them.

I knew that this school would need the same vision as Fitzsimons and Rhodes in order to make it a school. I had been the principal of Rhodes and Fitzsimons, and knew the students, families, and communities there well. I grew up in the same poverty-stricken neighborhood, and had attended poor schools in the same community. At Fitzsimons, I discovered what the vision for schools in poverty should entail. At Rhodes, I discovered that successful mergers are possible if the vision is clear and systems are formed. And as assistant superintendent, I solidified my notion that principals can change schools. I was prepared to lead a three-way merger into Strawberry Mansion High School; that is why it was my assignment.

I made it back to my office, sat in my blue leadership chair, and planned my final meeting with my 52 principals. In June, I told them I would be leaving in order to lead Strawberry Mansion High School. I told them that the children of those three schools were my responsibility, and that I had to make sure they were safe and educated. Some started to cry, because they knew I cared about them and my position, but that the children were my primary responsibility. I told them that if I was going to lead, I had to lead by example. They were my responsibility, just like their students were their responsibility. I further explained that leadership was complicated and purpose-driven. When you lead with purpose, you will find personal fulfillment on your own terms.

On July 1, 2012, I packed several boxes and relocated to Strawberry Mansion High School. I did not personally carry my blue leadership chair with me, as I had when I departed from Rhodes. I was a little sad to leave a job I loved, and I did not feel like carrying the chair down the long hallway to my van. I allowed them to move my chair for me with my belongings to signal the end of my position as assistant superintendent. I wanted the blue leadership chair to be waiting for me when I arrived at Strawberry Mansion High School, symbolizing my unwavering leadership and dedication to the students in that community.

I needed to see something empowering when I arrived for the first time back in my role as principal.

I was assigned to LEAD, and that was just what I planned to do.

## Thinking About Your Leadership

Looking back on my decision to leave the classroom after nearly 20 years to become a new teacher coach, and thinking about how I ended up as a principal two months later, I realize that the experience was all for a bigger plan in the future.

Look back over your own leadership journey. You will see signs that you were prepared for your mission. Take notes and connect the dots. A well-designed picture will appear, leading you to your greatest turnaround effort to date.

**Examine Attentively:** Your preparedness for your greater mission.

**Questions for You:**

- Are your leadership moves leading you to your real purpose in life?
- Are you committed to the overall mission even if you have to see it from another seat on the bus?

# 11

# Audacity

When I pulled up to Strawberry Mansion High School on July 1, 2012, I could not bring myself to get out of the car. I stared at the building from the parking lot across the street. As I sat there, I watched the children playing and walking down the street, and I could not help asking God why I had to come here. Condemned houses lined the streets, and I knew that there were families living in those condemned houses because they had nowhere else to go. Trash was everywhere, and there were young adults standing on every corner with nothing to do. I wondered whether any of those young adults were my students.

I had spent my entire career trying to get young people to escape poverty because I knew firsthand what poverty entailed. I had worked very hard to create a middle-class life for my family, but I could not escape "poverty" because helping others combat it had become my assignment. Watching children live in poverty each day was painful for me. It brought back so many memories. But knowing that my work could help a child escape from poverty energized me every day. That thought prompted me to get out of the car and slowly walk across the street. I had made the decision to lead Strawberry Mansion, but I could not help feeling a little depressed. If I had to pinpoint the source of my depression, I would have to say I felt powerless. Coming off the heels of supervising 52 principals to leading one school was a difficult shift to make.

I reached to open the front door to the school and found it locked. All of the others I tried were locked as well. I pulled, and pulled, and then tried to open them with a key I had been given. They still would not open. I called Ms. Jackson, who had followed me to Strawberry Mansion. She told me that I had to use the back door, because there were chains on the front door. While inspecting the front of the building, I noticed that the visitor sign was missing. You could see the light spot on the wall where it once was displayed. It did not mean anything at the time; I just made note of it.

As I drove my car around back to enter the rear of the school, something inside me did not feel right. Coming through the back door made me feel violated, belittled, and unimportant. Why were the children coming in the back door? What was wrong with the front door? Upon entering, I noticed that there was a visitor sign on the back entrance. Were the visitors coming through the back door as well? Teachers, parents, and guests?

When I finally entered the school, I had a flashback to Fitzsimons. I heard in my head "Miss, Miss, this is not a school" once more. It was as dark as night in the hallways. There were rows and rows of artificial plants that had not been dusted in years. There were old, faded bulletin boards posted on the wall, and student artwork that must had been there for years based on the fading of the paper. There were piles and piles of trash and broken furniture in almost every classroom. Central office had stored materials in unused classrooms. There was soiled carpet in a few classrooms, and classrooms with outside phone lines. The glass in the main office had not been cleaned since its installation in 1961. You could not stand inside the office and see the hallway from the inside. The glass was that dirty. The main office had cubicles that prevented the secretary from seeing someone standing at the counter. They were installed in such a way that they could never be taken down without major rewiring.

It was all so overwhelming, but it was the lack of light that took me over the edge. The poor lighting had caused the things I mentioned to go unnoticed. You could only see them if you were up close and personal. It was that dark. I went to the phone and called the facilities supervisor. As if I were still the assistant superintendent, I starting yelling at a man who answered the phone, "Get out here now! How in the world can I run a school when I cannot see?" I felt comfortable screaming at the facilities supervisor, because I knew all of the central office players not just as a principal, but as their equal. I made myself a promise that I if I was going to take on this merger, the district would keep every promise they made to this community to make this merger a reality. And it was going to start with the installation of new lights.

The sight of that building on my first day was so upsetting that all I could do after touring it was to look for my blue leadership chair. It was not in the main office. There were piles and piles of boxes to look through, because all the materials from the merged schools had also been delivered to Strawberry Mansion. I searched everywhere and asked everyone for my blue chair. It could not be found. I started to panic. I told everyone that they had to search for my blue chair.

I had my special assistant call central office to see whether it had been delivered. They responded that they had delivered it, but where was it? That chair had come to represent my leadership, and without it I was starting to question my whole decision. I started asking God, "Why me? I am one person—how in the world can I do anything with a place like this? Why is this my assignment?" But I quickly got myself together and called Ms. Jackson to walk with me once more to find my chair. I took my anger out on all of the faded bulletin boards and artificial trees. With every step I took, I started ripping down every outdated, faded piece of paper from the walls. Piles of dust filled the air. Then I turned my attention to the dirty, unkempt artificial trees. One by one, I threw them in the dumpster. I moved the few that remained out of the dark hallway and placed them in the bright foyer of the entryway, where there was plenty of light. I asked the cleaning staff to clean them thoroughly.

Standing in the foyer prompted me to ask Ms. Jackson about the chains on the school's front door. The previous administration had told her that the students did not use the front entrance of the school. Everyone used the back door because Ridge Avenue was a main road, and the previous administration did not want the children portraying a negative image in front of the school. So the decision was made to chain up the front doors, move the visitor sign from the front door to the back door, and have everyone enter through the rear of the school.

After that explanation, I called for the building engineer and told him to cut every lock off the chains on the front door. Then I asked him to go to the back door and bring the visitor sign back to the front of the building. I added more clean plants to the beautiful foyer at the front of the school, which had a high ceiling, ceramic tile walls and floors, and a beautiful picture of Dr. Ruth Wright Hayre—the first African American high school teacher and principal in Philadelphia, the first African American public school superintendent, and the first female president of Philadelphia's Board of Education. Strawberry Mansion and L.P. Hill had been named the Dr. Ruth Wright Hayre Educational Complex in her honor, but almost no one knew that. The name was changed by a mayoral proclamation in prior years. We were to call it Strawberry Mansion High School at the Dr. Ruth Wright Hayre Educational Complex. New name, new beginning.

After my display of rage was over, I returned to my office. And there it was—my blue leadership chair. It had been found among the piles and piles of deliveries. I closed my door, sat in my chair, and thought about my life in poverty, my students' lives in poverty, and the only way my mom taught me to escape it—through education. That day, I told myself that I would take on the role of mother to every one of my students, and fight for them to get an education and find a way out of poverty. That is why I was sent to Strawberry Mansion High School.

When a representative came out from the facility department, they had excuse after excuse for why there were no lights in the hallway in Strawberry Mansion High School. I was not listening to any of them. I refused to accept any answer but the date for installation. I insisted that I receive light before the students entered in September. I made all kinds of threats and painted horrible outcomes if we didn't get the lights. I even said, "No wonder this school had violent crime. You could not see it happening." After they realized that I would not take no for an answer, the real story about the lights emerged. Strawberry Mansion High School was funded for capital improvement, specifically for the lighting. Why were they never installed? Why did I have to fight for something that was already allocated to the school?

Day after day during the summer of 2012, I made demand after demand from the folks at central office. They cleaned the windows in the office for the first time since 1961. After the lighting was installed and the windows were clean, we discovered beautiful murals on the walls of the school that told many historical stories. A crew from central office replaced the soiled carpet on the floors, removed all of the stored materials, and cleaned the trash out of every classroom. They also sent us an additional metal detector so that we could open the beautiful front of the school safely to students, parents, and visitors.

On my first day at Strawberry Mansion High School, my emotions ran the gamut. I felt a sense of loss for my old position in the district and depressed that I had to make the decision to accept the challenge. I felt angry that it was my assignment and disgusted by the deplorable conditions I had found. But I also felt inspired by what the school could become and joyful that I had accepted the position to work at central office so that I was in a position to make demands that could make a difference. I was determined to make conditions conducive for learning for the 800 expected students who would come to Strawberry Mansion, and grateful that I did not have to enter Strawberry Mansion High School the same way I went into Fitzsimons: alone, and without a team.

## Thinking About Your Leadership

I made the decision to lead Strawberry Mansion. I was prepared for the mission, but it would take the audacity of bold leadership to set in on the right course. Bold leadership requires you to listen, but never accept excuses for why change cannot happen. Bold leadership requires you to jumpstart the change that is needed and insist that others do their part until the mission is complete. Bold leadership requires the willingness to make changes immediately for the good of the organization, even if they are small changes. Small changes represent new beginnings. Bold leadership requires the ability to stand up to anyone who has the power to give you what you need to make your mission successful. Bold leadership requires that you communicate effectively to get what you need to win the war.

**Examine Attentively:** Characteristics of **bold** leadership.

**Questions for You:**

- Are you practicing what is required when leading boldly?
- Have you thought about what you would say to get what you need for your organization?

# 12

# Seek

The first day at Strawberry Mansion was horrifying. The only thing that I was looking forward to on day two was the meeting my executive assistant set up for me and the leadership team. I had received the following email from a contact at the city mayor's office on June 20, 2012, while still in the assistant superintendent's chair, and I was eager to follow up:

> Hi Linda,
>
> I met with representatives from the city's Managing Director Office today. They work with communities to address issues identified by community members and leaders to bring city and other resources to the neighborhood to help resolve problems plaguing the community. They mentioned that Strawberry Mansion is one of their high priority areas of focus. They have done some work in the community but not in the high school. They are particularly interested in working with the high school around anti-violence initiatives. They have a working relationship with the US Attorney General's Office, and are very interested in working with Strawberry Mansion in light of the merging of two neighborhood high schools—the very issue you addressed in our meeting. They would like to meet with you whenever you are ready. . . . I hope you find this a helpful lead.

After deciding to go to Strawberry Mansion High School, I had been very vocal in my concerns about the violence that was likely to surround the merger. I had firsthand knowledge of all the discipline problems with the students, and I was told that a gun was brought into Strawberry Mansion High School in previous years.

After receiving the email, my executive assistant set up a meeting with all the people mentioned in the message. I added a few people from my leadership team, and they in turn added people from Town Watch.

The meeting was held in the principal's office. There was a huge boardroom table in the room and everyone had to squeeze in just to be able to sit at the table. I was very impressed by the response to the call for the meeting and elated that so many people wanted to help, but I was a little guarded with my emotions because I had seen this before. Everyone comes to the first meeting to hear about what is needed, and after the meeting no one returns to assist with the work. But I told myself to just get the help that I could now, and worry about the rest later. I was so overwhelmed by the pressure to keep everyone safe that I was willing to push total strangers to get what I needed to protect the staff and my students, even if it made me seem bossy.

Throughout my leadership career, I have always remembered valuable lessons taught by others in leadership positions and have never hesitated to put them into practice. One lesson I learned in particular came from a previous superintendent. He used to tell all the principals, "If you need something, tell somebody before something bad happens. If they do not help you, their heads will roll; but if you do not ask and something happens, your head is going to roll." I never forgot that lesson and it has served me well over the years. This was one of my major ask-for-support days, and I was not ashamed at all. I had lives to protect, a mission to carry out, and a purpose to fulfill.

The agenda for the meeting included all of the information I needed to gather and all the support I would need.

We had a meaningful discussion about the agenda items and recapped next steps. Everyone agreed that there was cause

# STRAWBERRY MANSION HIGH SCHOOL

Anti-Violence Meeting
July 2, 2012
9:00 a.m.–10:30 a.m.


## AGENDA

Meeting Facilitator: Linda Cliatt-Wayman, Principal, Strawberry
Mansion High School

| Welcome Attendees | Linda Cliatt-Wayman |
|---|---|
| I. Introductions | All |
| II. Reason for meeting<br>• The "big picture"<br>• Facilities Master Plan—<br>what is it?<br>• Desired meeting goals<br>(actionable plans)<br>• The need for community support | Linda Cliatt-Wayman |
| III. Discussion regarding current<br>community issues<br>• Past and current<br>conflicts/tensions<br>• Rivals? Which blocks? Codes,<br>signals, and tags? | Linda Cliatt-<br>Wayman, Attendees |
| IV. Discussion regarding anti-<br>violence initiatives and support<br>• What current anti-violence<br>supports are in place to handle<br>conflicts?<br>• What anti-violence initiatives can<br>be put in place?<br>• Who can SMHS rely on?<br>• Safe corridors | Linda Cliatt-<br>Wayman, Attendees |

| V. Facilitation of group meetings over the summer<br>• Student leaders<br>• Student orientations—ninth grade, continuing students | Linda Cliatt-Wayman, Attendees |
|---|---|
| VI. Additional questions, concerns | All |
| VII. Meeting recap/ Future plans | Linda Cliatt-Wayman |
| VIII. Meeting adjournment | Linda Cliatt-Wayman |

for concern with the merger. And everyone at the table offered an action to address the issue of violence on the agenda items. The meeting was adjourned, and dates for follow-up meetings were shared.

After every community member left the room, my leadership team and I remained at the table. A heavy sense of doom filled the room. No one said it, but we were all thinking it. The executive assistant to the U.S. Attorney for the Eastern District of Pennsylvania had given us the sobering statistics about the violence in the neighborhood. Why had we decided to come to Strawberry Mansion? Four members from my assistant superintendent team had accompanied me there. Of those four members, two had accompanied me from Fitzsimons to Rhodes to central office to Mansion. One had accompanied me from Rhodes to central office to Mansion, and another had accompanied me from central office. Their reason for putting themselves into this situation with me at Mansion was because they believed in my leadership and my mission. I sat there at the table silently thinking about the lessons I had learned when I became a leader a long time ago: it's the leader's responsibility to think of a plan of action with the resources at his or her disposal at the time of implementation. I never created a plan using resources that I thought were on the way. I had to create a plan with the people who sat around the table now. The leadership team and

I had to rely on each other and if additional help came, that is what it would be: additional help. The team and I sat there and considered everything we had heard from the violence presentation. We talked about what was being done and what we should anticipate based on what we had learned.

While the team was deep into planning, I received an email from the one person I was sure I would never hear from again. At the time of the meeting, I even wondered why he would attend a meeting about a high school when his current job at the U.S. Department of Justice was executive assistant to the United States District Attorney.

The email read as follows:

Mrs. Wayman,

Thanks so much for meeting with me this morning. It was eye-opening, refreshing, and inspiring to once again see the passion and energy you bring to your position, and to the students, teachers, and parents at Strawberry Mansion. I better understand the enormous challenges you face and appreciate the substantial effort it will take to reverse these issues that have been years in the making.

I want you to know that I am going to do what I can to support you and the school through the programs we discussed.

In my opinion, these should be relatively simple to achieve if we can get the buy-in from people in the school district. Over the past year, I have developed unprecedented, excellent relationships with the school district. Also, because I (my office) was asked to work at Strawberry Mansion, I believe they would be very open to seriously taking action on these issues. Please let me know if you are okay with my reaching out to the school district to discuss these issues.

I am very excited about our collaboration, and am optimistic that we will have profound impact on a number of students.

The US Attorney General's office was dedicated to helping a school in crisis. Usually, when people think of the U.S.

Attorney General's office in this community, they think about putting people in jail for a very long time. This time, they were coming to prevent crimes from happening. Their participation in the merger made me feel a lot of relief, but it also gave me a deeper perspective. This undertaking was more dangerous than I originally thought. I was so grateful for the follow-up email, and for the pledge of support.

My second day at Strawberry Mansion ended like my first: sitting in my blue leadership chair, thinking about all I had heard at the meeting. I was somewhat relieved to learn that my fears were warranted. They were not made up. They were not overemphasized. They were not in my head. The email was a confirmation to me that I was not going crazy. What I was about to walk into was dangerous for everyone. Why didn't I think about that before I decided to take the job? It was too late to worry about that. I had to look forward and finish devising a plan. I had to lead.

## Thinking About Your Leadership

Leaders think ahead about the mission. Leaders take the opportunity to ask questions and elicit support from familiar and unlikely people. When leaders meet with possible supporters, they have an idea of what they need. They are prepared. They know how to start the conversation. They know how to lead people into action. They know that the only people they can really depend on are themselves and the team, and if anyone else contributes, it is a bonus. Leaders learn from other leaders and listen to important things that other leaders share. Take lessons from what other leaders are saying, and make them a part of what you believe and what you will implement. When engaged in a turnaround mission, support is always needed. Embrace it, use it, seek it, and make sure the support is grounded in the overall mission of what you are trying to accomplish.

**Examine Attentively:** Your ability to identify and locate the resources needed for a successful turnaround mission.

**Questions for You:**

- How will you seek support for your turnaround mission?
- Are you prepared to forge ahead without additional support?

# 13

# Listen

After the team met with the community leaders, we were more concerned than ever about the merger. The danger that loomed ahead consumed us every day. Talk of guns and violence weighed on our minds constantly. The leadership team was set. Only four additional team members joined the team prior to the school opening. Ms. Jackson was the only member of the team who had taken my entire leadership journey with me. There were nine members on the team again. The perfect size. The perfect team that would take on the impossible. We had one goal—"make it a school"—a school free from violence, a place to learn and grow academically, ensuring that our students would be successful adults.

The first line of business was to meet and strategize after the meeting with the community leaders. We were hoping for their support when school opened, but we could not depend on it. So we forged ahead with our plan for success. We spent hours designing an implementation plan. We noted all of the things that needed to be addressed. There were so many things that we grew weary just thinking about them.

After meeting with the community leaders, our second line of business was to meet with parents of the students who would be affected by the merger. We did not know what to expect, so we planned for the worst. The meeting was held in a classroom on the second floor. Some of the students came to the meeting with their parents. The parents were not friendly at all. They were downright rude. They wanted to know how I was going to keep the violence down. They wanted to know about the school uniforms. They wanted to know what I was going to do about books and other materials. They wanted to know what I was going to do about everything, and they did not say anything about what they were going to do. Their tone was offensive and disrespectful, but I did not take it personally. They were just angry that their children had to attend Strawberry Mansion. Angry, and scared.

I had an agenda. Most of the parents present had children with special needs. They were especially concerned about safety. I was surprised to have one of my special needs teachers present at the meeting. She suggested that she take all of the children, and I was glad she did. I could now focus on the parents, and the parents could focus on their questions. They questioned everything (and they should!), but in the back of my mind I wanted to ask, "Where were you when they were deciding whether the school should relocate or close? Where were you with all of your questions at the multiple community meetings around the merger?" I was present at all of them, and I never met one of these parents. But it was time to listen to them now. Their children would be intimately involved in this merger, and they had the right to some answers.

What they did not know was that the plan was being created less than two months in advance of the school opening. They thought the "district" had given me this grand plan. If they only knew that there were nine people trying to make it happen with what we had researched, rehearsed, and previously experienced, they would have been scared out of their minds. So I did not tell them. I told them the parts of the plan that they were mainly interested in. One of the main things they were interested in was the uniform. This raised a lot of noise. The parents from the three different schools yelled and screamed about buying new uniforms to attend Strawberry Mansion. They kept repeating they already had uniforms from their other schools, and they were not buying any more. They argued and argued. I thought they were going to break out into a fight. Finally, to increase the tension, one parent said with authority, "We are not buying any more uniforms and you cannot make us."

Can you imagine what it would be like if the three rival schools wore their own school colors to the new school? I had nightmares that they would fight each other all day just because they had on different colors. It was the team's thinking that the students who attended Rhodes and Fitzsimons could easily be identified in their school colors and would be picked on and bullied every day by the Mansion students. At the meeting, the Mansion students were the most vocal, saying things like, "They better not wear those Rhodes or Fitzsimons shirts up in here. That is not going to happen."

My team and I had anticipated school uniforms being a problem. So, to reassure the parents, I told them that they did not have to buy any new uniforms. They started high fiving each other and saying in a nasty tone, "told you we were not buying any new uniforms," as if they won the first battle with me and my team. They assumed they were going to be allowed to wear the uniforms from Fitzsimons and Rhodes. Instead, I told the Strawberry Mansion parents that their children could not wear their Mansion uniform. They all looked puzzled. Then I broke the news that the Rhodes and Fitzsimons students were not wearing their former school uniforms to Mansion either. Everyone was confused until I explained that none of the three schools would be wearing their old school uniforms when the doors opened in September. They all had to wear what we called "school appropriate attire": collared shirts, pants or skirts, and shoes or sneakers only. No tights, leggings, liquid pants, belts, saggy pants, or hoodies. We chose this attire because we did not want any child singled out based on the school they attended previously. We did not want any child to be a target. We made it very simple, or so we thought.

The parents screamed even louder. "That is stupid! Why can't our kids wear the uniforms? I am not buying any new clothes!" Even though we told the parents that it was a safety concern, they still wanted their children to wear the uniforms they had. I told them in a very forceful voice how that was not going to happen. No students would be walking into Strawberry Mansion with a Fitzsimons, Rhodes, or Mansion logo written across their shirts. That would only cause problems. I made that decision, and that was that.

After all of the noise over the uniforms had died down, it was time to take the parents on a tour of the school. Before going on the tour, one parent yelled out in a nasty tone, "What are you going to do about the school having no books?" I asked them where they got the idea that this school had no books. Several parents agreed and said that their child never brought home any books, and that it was because there were no books used in the classroom. I told the parents the school had plenty of books, and the yelling and screaming among the parents started again. "There are no books in this school!" Even the students joined in and said "There are no books in the school!" When the students started yelling that there were no books, I was very confused. My only recourse to get them to stop yelling and screaming at me was to show them the books. I said to my team member who was giving the tour: "Let's make our first stop on the tour the book closet in the basement of the school." That was the largest book closet, but one of many. When I opened the door for the parents to walk inside, their mouths opened wide. Many of them, along with the children, stared as they looked around, saying, "Oh my God. Look at all these books," as if they had never seen a book in the school. One student even ran over to the dictionaries and said, "My teacher told us we had no dictionaries." I stood there, frozen, listening and watching in disbelief. I felt so sad inside. They really thought there were no books in the school. Then in unison, all of the parents and students pulled out their cell phones saying, "We have to take pictures and videos of this. We cannot believe this." They filmed and filmed, and took picture after picture. I wanted to cry. What was I getting myself into? Did I really know?

Why had no one ever taken the time to show the students they had books in the school? Why weren't the teachers using the books that were there? Why did the parents send their children to school day after day without demanding to see a book? I could only let those thoughts cross my mind for a minute, before returning to the joyful moment before me. The students and parents were elated because the school had books. It was the first time I had seen them smile since they walked in the door of the school for the meeting. The first time that there was positive noise, not yelling and screaming and combative behavior. I wanted them to go home happy, not fearful of the merger. I took the opportunity to end the parent and community meeting there in the book closet on a high, joyous note.

## Thinking About Your Leadership

As leaders, you must practice the art of listening. Listening to all stakeholders and involving everyone in the process is crucial to the mission. You never want to hear "I did not know" from anyone.

However, sometimes listening to all sides will not bring about a consensus. Sometimes you (as the leader) will have to make decisive calls. It may be uncomfortable, but you are the expert. After listening to all sides and integrating what others think with your experiences, you have to know you are the best person to make the ultimate decision for the good of the organization. That is what leadership is all about.

While listening to others, you may discover new information that can be crucial to the planning process. The information could be true or false, but it is worth investigating for the good of the organization. When something needs to be addressed, do so in a timely fashion; if you do not, it could ruin the culture of the workplace before the mission begins.

Finally, know when to end your listening sessions. Never end your listening sessions on a negative note. Meetings that end on a negative note will be counterproductive and everyone will leave the listening session unclear about the true essence of the meeting. It is appropriate to sometimes stray away from your agenda in order to keep things positive. You can easily revisit the remaining items at a later date. Ending your listening session on a positive note leaves everyone energized, eager, and focused only on the positives for the time being.

**Examine Attentively:** When you must make decisive calls after listening to all sides involved.

**Questions for You:**

- Does making the decision scare you? If so, why? Examine those reasons and address them.
- Are you ready to hear and address the perceptions in your organization?

---- 14 ----

# Customized

The summer of 2012 was now over. All of the community meetings were behind us. The meeting with the incoming teaching staff was over. It was time for our official leadership retreat. We met extensively throughout the summer, but these three days in August were set aside for us to review all of the plans we were about to implement on the first day of school. We had our own turnaround model to make Strawberry Mansion High a school. No directives came from central office. We had to figure it out ourselves because there was no example for us to follow. Yes, there were turnaround schools called "Promise Academies" in the district, but we were not considered one of those. We did not get any additional resources or a turnaround model to follow. We just had nine people who were committed to making a three-way high school merger a successful mission.

The Strawberry Mansion High School Turnaround Model was an extension of the three components we used to make Fitzsimons and Rhodes schools: building relationships, teaching and learning, and school safety. The Strawberry Mansion High School Turnaround Model consisted of the following components:

**A New Vision**
- A roster overhaul that included the reconfiguration of the lunch periods and the instructional periods. Time blocks were created to make room for seven classes (credits) a year

instead of six in each student's schedule to help with credit deficiencies.

- All English and math classes were gender-separate.
- All teachers returning to Strawberry Mansion were moved out of their existing classrooms to others. New teachers were carefully placed throughout the building in order to be supported, not tainted by disgruntled employees who were still angry about the change.
- Common planning time for teachers was built into the school-day schedule. This was very important because it was mandatory that the teachers plan together weekly.
- A mandated instructional delivery model was introduced. That included a seven-step format with small group instruction to aid in differentiation.
- An informal observation form was created to assist in collecting data for teacher feedback, with a focus on improving learning in the classroom
- An Honors program (which included dual enrollment in the Community College of Philadelphia), an Alternative Education Program, and a career and technical program were set up for implementation, along with general studies and various electives.
- A Non-Negotiable Schoolwide Discipline System was developed with steps for implementation, tracking, and intense follow-through.
- Formation of SAR. Student Accommodation Room. A designated space provided for student reflection and a strategy used to support teachers with discipline challenges to alleviate classroom disruptions
- A plan was developed to take student on several field trips outside of the North Philadelphia community.
- Monthly town hall meetings in the form of an assembly were established to hear students' voices and address concerns head on.
- Five core values to keep everyone motivated were stressed: Perseverance, Excellence, Focus, Tradition, and Integrity.

- School beautification was mandated around a particular monthly theme.
- Building positive relationships with students was a must. "Respect them and they will respect you" became my mantra.
- Daily announcements that would end with me saying, "If nobody told you they loved you today, remember I do, and I always will!"

At the leadership retreat, we ironed out all of the steps for the model's implementation. Who would do what, and what would that look like? We knew we had to get each part correct beginning the very first day of school or it would be a terrible school year. The part of the model that would make or break us was the rollout, unveiling, and implementation of the schoolwide discipline system. The system was of course called "Non-Negotiable Schoolwide Rules," just as at Rhodes, but there were a few slight variations to the system at Strawberry Mansion High School: "appropriate attire" replaced the uniform; opening exterior doors was prohibited; prevention of property vandalism, a major problem, was stressed; the use of only one stairwell; no hall walking or loitering; no physical or verbal assault or bullying; and cell phones had to be powered off.

The team had a lot of questions about the implementation of these rules and the students' anticipated reaction. How long was it going to take for the students to comply? What was going to force them to comply? At the onset, we did not plan to rid ourselves of the "persistently dangerous" label; we were just trying to stay alive and keep the staff and students safe in a dangerous school.

As I was sitting in my blue leadership chair with my team surrounding me, trying to fine-tune opening day, I could hear a women screaming at the secretary, "I just want to see the principal!" She was screaming so loudly that she interrupted the team's focus. I looked out of my office door (where she could not see me) and saw a woman there with her son. Her son's eyes were red and swollen to the point that they were almost closed. He did not look school age, had tattoos all over his neck, and seemed like he might be high or drunk. And he appeared totally disinterested in being at the school. While his mother was yelling, he said nothing. Unfortunately, because so many of the parents came to the school and demanded to see the principal in very offensive ways, I usually paused before going out to see any of them. I wondered how many screaming parents I would have to face in the near future at Strawberry Mansion.

Over the years, it has always been my aim to teach my parents how to interact appropriately when they go to their children's school. Many parents are used to getting their way with the school when they come in screaming, hollering, and using offensive language with the secretary. I never respond to a parent's demand to see me if they are using offensive language. So I immediately went into teaching mode with this parent. I stepped out of the office and asked, "Do you have an appointment with me?" She said no, this time with a more respectful tone, so I decided to invite her into my office. If she had continued screaming, demanding, and cursing, I would have asked my secretary to make her an appointment and refused to see her until she acted appropriately. Seeing her while acting inappropriately only validates such behavior, and each time she would go to the school she would act the same way to get the desired outcomes.

The team took a break and left the room. The woman came into my office, sat down with her son, and said, "Mrs. Wayman, I want my boy to go to school." As he sat there, looking high and totally uninterested, his mother went on to tell me about her other son and how well he was doing with his new career, wife, and job, and how she wanted the same for this son. This was her last child to put through school. After trying to get her son to say something and stop looking uninterested, his mother began to cry. She begged him to do what was right, stay out of trouble, and just go back to school. She told me he had been out of school for a year or two because a teacher accused him of assault when he was in the fifth grade. Every school they put him in was a disciplinary school. She did not like the disciplinary schools, so he stopped going to school briefly and now he was over 18. "Please," she pleaded through her tears, "help me save my son."

I had never met this person in my life, but she reminded me so much of my mother. She just wanted her son to graduate from high school. She went on to say: "I know you do not have to take him because he is already 18, but please Miss—help me help him." I looked at the young man and said, "Son, look at your mother. Look at her. Do you want to see her cry like this?" He then turned to his mother and said, "Mom, stop crying. Stop crying, Mom; I will come to school." I saw that he could feel the pain that his mother felt.

I thought about the new program we had just developed in our turnaround model: the Alternative Education Program. The program would consist of daily counseling, a later arrival time and early departure time, and blended learning classes that were self-paced and had two classroom assistants to help with students with special needs. The program also included lunch and physical education, and one special teacher to oversee it all in an isolated wing in the building in order for the students to stay focused. It was designed for students who were overaged and under-credited, just like this young man. I told the mother that we could put her son in this program, but that he would have to cooperate in order to remain. I looked directly at him, and told him that he better come to school—if not for himself, then for his mother.

That day, the team and I knew that our Alternative Education Program would be desperately needed in Strawberry Mansion High School. We were elated that it was part of our model. We had it all figured out on paper, but we had to wait to see whether it would work in practice. It was a risk we had to take. We made a vow to enroll every student who was mature enough to handle the program until they were 21 years old.

As I sat in my blue leadership chair and reflected on our preparations to open, I was confident that we had planned for every anticipated challenge ahead, as well as a few unanticipated problems that we might encounter. The team tried to think of everything that could possibly go wrong on the first day of school and beyond, and address these concerns in advance. We had developed as a leadership team with clearly defined roles and a vision to inspire our work "to save lives"; we had met with all stakeholders; we had formulated and strategized implementation for the turnaround model for change; we had asked for assistance, but did not count on it; and we prayed that all of our hard work and preparation during the summer would pay off.

The staff attended two days of professional development in early September before school was set to officially open. During the two-day professional development, the executive assistant from the U. S. Department of Justice had provided the staff with all of the awful numbers about crime in the Strawberry Mansion area, including the death rate of school-age children in the area and the frequency of gun possession. That professional development session was graphic enough to scare anyone.

The teachers were also given an overview of the turnaround model the leadership team had developed. Every teacher was given his or her new classroom assignment; novice and seasoned teachers alike would have classrooms. The students were walking into something new and had to adjust to change, and so did the staff. Changing classrooms gave everyone an immediate sign that it was not going to be business as usual. Teachers were given a new framework for teaching, compliance rules for lesson plan submission, and a review of the existing data. Formal and informal observation protocol, a review of the Non-Negotiable Schoolwide Discipline System, and the professional development calendar were introduced for some and reviewed for others. The teachers were informed about every expectation.

The professional development also ended with a reminder. With deep concern, I told the teachers that we were all parents, grandparents, aunts, and uncles, and that if we were all going to go home safe each night, we would have to follow the plan set for the school's turnaround and work together. I needed for everyone to go home well-informed about the role they would play in making this merger a success.

The staff departed for the day, but the leadership team remained well into the evening (many hours past our set departure time). We talked about the plans once more, and prepared to leave. As we were leaving, I looked at the exterior door and remembered one last task that had to be completed before the first day of school: posting signs. Bright neon green signs were posted on every single door that led outside. They read: "STOP! Think about opening these doors. It will result in a five-day suspension." Fear of guns entering the school had prompted me to post these signs. Extreme measures for an extreme situation. We were now ready to open!

## Thinking About Your Leadership

Do not go into an organization thinking you have to overhaul and change it all at once. And don't panic! There are some existing ideas, strategies, and plans that you can build on when you arrive. Think about things you have done in the past that were successful practices, combine them with parts of an already viable plan, and use that as a springboard to create and implement new projects. Research what others have done in similar situations. Use the parts you think work, and then enhance them with your own new ideas. Adding to the blueprint of what you already know works will make your new "big thing" look manageable and possible.

**Examine Attentively:** Your custom model for success.

**Questions for You:**

- Do you know how to customize a turnaround model using research, your experiences, and your gut feelings?
- Are you aware that leaders must use unconventional methods and take risks in order to turn around a failing organization? Nothing will change if you don't go for it!

# 15

# Strength

On September 10, 2012, I arrived at school at 6:45 a.m. I sat in my blue leadership chair and wondered whether I had prepared everything for my main goal to be accomplished: to keep the students and staff safe in the midst of this difficult merger. I was mainly thinking about my girls from Rhodes. They would be the most vulnerable. They were also the ones who had been given false promises that were then snatched away, leaving them in this horrible situation. I partly blamed myself. I should have been able to protect them and give them what was promised, but I was not. My love for them became my tangible reason to come to Strawberry Mansion High School. Every decision I made was made with them in mind. Yes, I wanted to "make it a school." But first I wanted to keep them physically safe, and in doing so, create an environment for all of the students to grow and learn.

As I sat there in my blue chair waiting anxiously for the school bell to ring, I found myself getting angry. Angry with myself for being in this situation. Angry with the parents of the children assigned to this school for not advocating for their children's education. Angry at the rumors about how the students would behave, which just encouraged that behavior. Angry at the school district for using the reason of facility usage to put 800 students from rival schools into one building. Angry at all involved for creating a situation that no sane person would go into as principal.

Angry at everyone for the condition the building was in when I arrived. Angry for my involvement in this unbelievable plan. I was angry about pretty much everything. I sat there and closed my eyes and prayed to God that what we had done to keep the students and staff safe was enough.

All of my trials and tribulations had groomed me for this moment to take on this task. My anger subsided quickly. I wiped the tears from my eyes. I was not sure of the magnitude of the task, but I was absolutely sure that it was my assignment.

I recapped my preparations in my mind and emerged from the confines of my office feeling confident and strong and totally prepared for whatever the day might bring. I stood at the front counter in the main office and greeted my leadership team members as they arrived. They were all somber, trying desperately to mentally prepare themselves for what they had signed up for. All of them loved the children and the mission, but none of them would have accepted the challenge if I had not asked them to be a part of it. It was my purpose and leadership that they trusted. I showed them I was ready by questioning each one of them about the memo a teammate had sent out regarding the leadership team's first-day assignments. I asked each of them to explain to me one more time what task they were responsible for handling. As always, they all were armed with the correct answers. They knew what they had to do, and they owned it.

After each team member had reviewed his or her assignment with me, I returned to my office to review the deployment plan. I wanted to make sure that I was correctly utilizing all of my climate support. I had been over this plan time and time again, but I wanted to check it one last time. With the school budget, I had hired 13 hall monitors, two climate managers, and a conflict resolution specialist. Central office had assigned six school police officers and a police sergeant to help manage the officers. When the sergeant came to the school two days before school opened, he said it was his job to create the deployment plan for his officers and direct their whereabouts, and that if the deployment plan needed adjusting he would adjust it. After he explained his duties, I handed him the deployment plan for his officers and the entire climate staff. I told him that it was not going to be his job to create a deployment plan because he did not take the time to come to the school to plan in advance. There was no way for him to do in two days what had taken me two months to create. I told him that I was the principal, and that every person in the building was my responsibility, including his officers. I asked him to review it so that he would become familiar with it, but he was not to change anything unless I gave him permission. He was not very happy about that. I included the sergeant as part of the safety team. There would not be one person over the officers. Everyone was part of one team. That first meeting with the sergeant was intense, but I meant what I said. The climate of that building was my responsibility, and I was relinquishing it to no one . . . especially someone I met two days before the opening of school.

To round out the safety team, two armed Philadelphia police officers were assigned to the school. Even though we had a vast safety team, it did not feel like a prison. I made sure of that. All personnel were deployed strategically so that the students would not feel overwhelmed by the police presence. Ninety-four surveillance cameras captured everything, adding a final layer of protection. It was a school in the making, not a prison in the making. When I met with the entire climate team prior to opening the doors for the first time, I reminded them that Strawberry Mansion was a school, not a beat, and that there would be no aggression with the students unless it was warranted. (That was another complaint the students had mentioned during our summer meeting—that the police treated them unfairly—so I wanted to address that concern early on). Many of the officers did not like my approach to school discipline. They kept reminding me that the students were dangerous. I responded by saying that not all of them were dangerous, and they all should be treated with respect and dignity until they gave us a reason to treat them otherwise. I wanted them to know that was a directive, not a request. The officers didn't realize that I had put a protocol in place to watch how they treated the students. I told my two climate managers to always listen to the walkie-talkie, and that if any students were placed in police custody, they were to report to the holding location and remain there until the students were released. This was my way of letting the officers know that I meant what I said. No child would be put into handcuffs without reason, no child would be placed in harm's way without just cause, and no child would be bullied by the police. When the police noticed this practice, they were not happy about it; but it kept them in compliance, and that was the goal.

All of the police officers were very good at their jobs. I soon discovered that they were patient, kind, and very concerned for the welfare of all the students. Each officer was unique and had different strengths. One officer stood out from the rest. He was always calm, collected, and positive. He never raised his voice above a whisper, and spoke very little. I knew that I was going to place him at the front door to greet all of the visitors because of his pleasant smile and calm demeanor. Before the school bell rang on that first day, they were all in position as directed by the deployment plan. It was my climate manger's job to make sure everyone was in compliance with the plan, and it was my job to make sure that communication was always open to make adjustments as needed.

After I had checked the deployment plan and met with the climate team, I walked back to the office counter to watch the teachers as they arrived for opening day. Some looked worried, and some looked annoyed by the changes. The teaching staff was split. Half of the staff was new to the school and the other half was from the old regime. However, we were one staff about to embark on a new venture together. Everyone and everything was now in place. All of the preparation was officially over. We had planned up until the very last minute. As the time drew near for the bell to ring, I went back into my office and stood next to my blue leadership chair. I closed my eyes to pray one last time. I only said one line: "God, give me strength."

The school bell sounded. It was time to let the students inside and wait for them to make their move. It was like a chess game.

We had made most of our moves before the game even began. But little did they know, I was saving my other moves for after they disclosed their initial move. I had to make this school a safe place to learn.

## Thinking About Your Leadership

In life we all hear the inner voice that tells us what our focus should be. At times we resist that voice in order to do things our way. Every turnaround leader is faced with the question, "Will you lead or not?" Leading through difficult times takes FAITH. Seeing success when it is not visible to others takes FAITH. When you lead through a turnaround situation armed with a source of strength and clear reason for why you were chosen to lead, you will lead successfully. Have faith that *you* are the one for the job and go do it.

**Examine Attentively:** The source of your strength to LEAD.

**Questions for You:**

- Do you really believe that you have been prepared to lead the mission you are currently undertaking?
- Do you have the strength and the faith to lead your mission to success?

# 16

# Relentless

When the school bell rang at 8:00 a.m., it was time to open the doors to let the students inside. Before any student was allowed to walk through the door to approach the body scan machine or the metal detectors, my climate manager was on his post for his first assignment, as the town crier. It was his job to go outside and remind the students to look inside their pockets and bags for anything that might be inappropriate to bring into a school. He yelled with a bullhorn, "Hear ye, hear ye! Empty your pockets! Check your bags! You are entering a building that is secure with officers, state-of-the-art metal detectors, and body scan machines, so please make sure you have no weapons or drugs in your pockets. Weapons and drugs are prohibited in the school building. If you bring in those items, you will be arrested. What are weapons? Weapons are knives, guns, scissors, razors, and metal or wooden objects. You know what drugs are not allowed: marijuana, crack, or cocaine." After repeating this several times over the loud voices of the students, the climate manager then moved away from the door for the students to enter, still repeating the same announcement for any new students who approached the door. He stayed out there for over an hour saying the same thing, "Empty your pockets, check your bags, please!"

As the students filed into the school, I stood in the middle of the hallway near stairwell D to direct their travel throughout the building to get their rosters. I had a smile on my face because

I was happy to see them, but I stood tall to let them know that I was not afraid to be at Mansion and I was not afraid of them. The entrance of stairwell D was a great location to greet, welcome, and inspect each student for uniform compliance. Uniform compliance was important to me. From past experiences, I knew that not sticking to the uniform policy was the students' first passive aggressive move made toward administration. In my mind I knew I had to win with uniform compliance.

As the students walked past me, I looked them up and down to make sure they were in compliance with the policy. Their parents had been told in person and through a phone chain the uniform policy over and over again. No uniform shirts from the three merged schools. They could wear any other shirt as long as it had a collar, and they had to wear pants with a belt, and no boots. Simple . . . or so I thought! As they filed in, many of the boys had on white t-shirts without collars, baggy pants with no belts in sight, and rags hanging from their back pockets. A few even tried to get in with the uniform shirt from their previous schools, but they never made it past the officers on the door. We knew that would start a war. So they were not allowed inside the school until they changed their shirts. This was simple for them to do. They had the appropriate attire in their possession. They were just checking to see whether we were going to follow our own rule. They were testing us.

I allowed everyone else to enter without interruption, even though they did not follow some variation of the policy. If they did not have a collared shirt, they were allowed inside the building. If they did not have on a belt and their underwear was visible, they were still allowed inside the school. There would be time to address non-compliance with the rule later. Their appearance startled many of my teachers, and evoked fear in some of them. Many of the students did not look like they were coming to school to learn, but instead to be part of a gang. And many of them looked like adults. One student had the nerve to come to school with the word "bitch" permanently tattooed on his face. I immediately called his parent and told her he was not getting into school looking like that. He transferred, and I never saw him again. The teachers saw that move as a sign that I was going to protect them.

On the other hand, many students did comply. They looked beautiful in their required attire. They just wanted to learn. I knew that those were the students I had to worry about the most. Among the students were several from Rhodes who had been unable to transfer to other schools. Their parents were clearly relieved to see that I was the principal and left their children there knowing that I would do my best to educate them and keep them safe. So many beautiful, innocent children coming to school to get an education. They all just looked so scared. All the extensive prepping was clearly made with them in mind. They deserved the opportunity to receive a quality education in their own neighborhood, free of fear. It became my primary responsibility to eliminate every barrier that would prevent learning from happening.

In the midst of my inspection of the dress code compliance, one parent came out of nowhere with her child and walked right up to me yelling, "I want my child out of here. I want my child out of here right now! She is not coming here." Her child, a former student of mine from Rhodes, reached around her and gave me a big hug. "Mrs. Wayman," she asked, "are you really the principal?" When I said yes, she turned to her mother and said, "Mom, if Mrs. Wayman is here, I will be fine." After asking her if she was sure, the girl replied "Yes," and the mother left her with me. That made me feel good, but more burdened at the same time. Could I really protect all of these children?

Just as I was reviewing in my mind what to say to the many students who did not follow the dress code on the first day of school, I heard one of the police officers urgently calling for me over the walkie-talkie. He told me I needed to come to the police holding area in a hurry. When I got there, one of my climate managers was already on the scene, where a well-dressed young man was handcuffed, and a very large amount of cash and marijuana was on the desk. I asked him where he got that, and why he had so much cash on him. With his head hanging down, his response was that he was going to buy school clothes after school. I then asked why he brought drugs into my school and he said, "I forgot that it was in my pocket." When I asked, "What are you doing with that large quantity of drugs?" he had no answer. Thank God the drugs were seized at the entrance during intake.

The police had to be called to transport the student to jail that very first day of school. All of the warnings did not help. The Town Crier did not help. He heard the call to empty his pockets. Why did he not comply? It was later determined that he came to school to sell the drugs. I guess he did not believe that Strawberry Mansion High School was going to be different. He went to jail and received a 10-day suspension. During the 10-day suspension, his disciplinary transfer papers were completed. He was assigned to a disciplinary school, and I never saw him again.

As the students continued to arrive, their schedules were distributed and they reported to their advisors to get important information and to review the schoolwide discipline system with their advisors. At 10:00 a.m., the advisors escorted their students to the auditorium for what would be our first town hall meeting. This was going to be my first time to address the students' non-compliance with the uniform policy, the drug confiscation, and my role as principal.

As the students filed into the auditorium, I immediately flashed back to my first day at Fitzsimons. It was déjà vu. The students entered talking very loudly, and the teachers had a very difficult time keeping the students all together. They would stop to talk with their friends in the middle of the auditorium, ignoring the teachers' requests to follow them and take a seat. There were no working microphones, so Ms. Jackson handed me a bullhorn. It took repeated calls through the bullhorn as I stood on stage for them to finally be seated. By the time they were finally seated and quiet enough for me to speak, I was annoyed. I was annoyed because I had to wait to get their attention. I was annoyed because I had no microphone. I was annoyed because I watched the students have total disregard for the wishes of their teachers to sit down and be quiet. I was annoyed because many students and their parents had ignored the call for appropriate uniform attire. I was annoyed because someone had the nerve to bring a large quantity of marijuana into my building on the first day of school after I had spent many, many hours trying not to have any student arrested. I was annoyed that some of the nicest students had to be subjected to fear in school. It was the first day of school, and I was annoyed! Annoyed that I had planned for the worst, and had ended up seeing it. I had to use every conventional and unconventional plan just to get through the first two hours of school.

Because I had so many things to be annoyed with, and because I wanted to create a safe space for the many children who had started the school year off right, I had to take control. I did not want them to go home and tell their parents that the students acted totally out of control, and that there was no one there to correct their behavior. I wanted them to go home and tell their parents that they would be alright because someone other than the students was in control.

I introduced myself as the principal, repeated my name about three times, and then put one hand on my hip while holding the bullhorn with the other. "I have no idea where you think you are," I began, "but in case you do not know where you are, let me explain to you that you are in my house. Yes, *my* house—and one day, I hope it will become *our* house. In case you do not understand what I mean when I say my house, let me paint you a little picture. You know in North Philadelphia, young men claim street corners. There are rules for claimed corners. I cannot tell anyone what to do on his or her corner because I do not know the rules of corner life. Do you understand? In case you do not, let me give you another scenario. What your family does in their house is their business. I cannot go in their house and tell them what to do. Why, because that is not my house. And I do not make the rules. Well, Strawberry Mansion High School is *my* house; and in my house, you follow my rules, and you will have no problems.

My staff stared at me in shock, but I had everyone's attention!

"Now that I have your attention, and before I have to make another arrest on the first day of school, let me tell you about the rules for my House: Strawberry Mansion High School. Your advisor should have introduced them to you, but I need you to hear them from me. Once you hear these rules face-to-face from me, they are the rules. Again, these rules are called non-negotiable rules." I read out the rules one-by-one, then continued. "Let's talk about what non-negotiable means. What is the definition for non-negotiable? Before I could tell you the rules myself, many of you had already broken two of them: the dress code policy and drugs on school grounds. Bringing drugs into my house is a non-negotiable. The punishment for breaking non-negotiable rules is an out-of-school suspension." At that point, a student yelled, "We do not care." I responded by saying, "You will when you cannot get in without your parent."

In the past, out-of-school suspensions were a joke. Students would be suspended, stay out of school for the days they were given, and just come back to school after they had served their days. The parent was never notified in writing, and the parent or guardian was never asked to come to the school to reinstate his or her child. So the students perceived it as a party. They walked the streets during the days they were suspended, then came back to school and caused havoc with no family member involved to help alter their behavior.

So I explained the new process for returning to school after being suspended for breaking a non-negotiable. The students would receive the suspension notice with the entire story typed on it for their parents to see. They would stay out the number of days given, and return with a parent or guardian for a conference. If the parent or guardian could not come to reinstate the child, they were allowed to place three additional people on the list to reinstate in their absence. It was important that someone knew the student had broken a rule.

As the process for reinstatement was being reviewed and all of the school rules were being spelled out, the students were still laughing, hollering, and making all kinds of noise. I continued to review the rules over the noise and told them that if they did not hear me, they had better read their handbooks—because after the town hall meeting was over and all of their questions were addressed, the rule was the rule. When a student yelled from the back, "Hey, Miss, we do what we want!" I responded, "Not in my house you don't."

It was clear that the students had never heard of school-wide rules and a system to make sure they stayed in compliance. No wonder Strawberry Mansion was dangerous. There had been no rules that the students actually had to follow. No standard of norms for how the entire school community should act with one another. They really believed it was appropriate for them to live by the mantra: "We do what we want."

There was nothing at the time that I could say or do to make them see things my way. I had to set the stage, and then prove to them I would win the war. I had no choice. The lives of children lay in the balance. It was their choice to be non-compliant with the uniform policy after repeated notices, their choice not to listen to their teachers, their choice to bring in drugs even though they were warned to check their pockets before entering. Now it was my time to implement and monitor all of the plans designed as a response to the behaviors we anticipated. My team and I had planned for a day such as this one. We were not going to be deterred. The children deserved to be educated in a safe space, and opposition was not going to take me off course. Instead, it fueled my need to win every battle and the war even more.

As the day came to a close, I retreated to my office and sat in my blue leadership chair. This was different for me. I was used to going outside with my students, walking them to the bus, or even standing on the bus stop corner with them, making small talk. But at Strawberry Mansion High School, that was not to be. When I headed for the door to walk outside at dismissal, my officers asked me to stay inside the building because it would be too difficult for them to protect me and the students outside. Then they said, "You must stay inside, because you do not have a bulletproof vest." I was shaken by that comment, so I stayed inside to prepare myself for a long battle. A battle I intended to win.

## Thinking About Your Leadership

Opposition to change will keep you up at night. It can come from a variety of sources, and it can be vicious. To lead through opposition, you must believe in your plan of action. You must be ready to make sudden adjustments along the way. You must address the opposition in a timely manner. If you do not address it, it will get worse. Your staff will look at your refusal to address opposition as a sign of weakness, and then they will make their takeover move in some fashion. Be confident, and be relentless. It will not be easy; however, victory will come if you have prepared.

**Examine Attentively:** Your relentless ability to stay the course when faced with opposition.

**Questions for You:**

- Do you know how to address opposition in a creative way?
- How can you use opposition to move you closer to your desired goal?

# 17

# Steadfast

I could not get the phrase "We do what we want" out of my mind. I really had a hard time understanding why so many of the students embraced the idea that Strawberry Mansion High School was a place where they could just come and do whatever they wanted to do. Where did that line of thinking come from? Who believes that they live in a world where they can just do what they want? No wonder Strawberry Mansion High School was on the National Persistently Dangerous list and had been for five consecutive years. That kind of thinking is dangerous. That is why the level of arrests due to assaults on teachers and students had outpaced most of the district. The community must have been aware of the mindset of the students assigned to Strawberry Mansion, because only 300 of the 800 students scheduled to attend Strawberry Mansion actually entered Mansion. Fear had caused many families to flee and refuse to send their children to a "persistently dangerous" school. I lost a lot of sleep worrying about where all the other students ended up. I just prayed they went to school somewhere. The forced closure of schools that came out of the Facility Master Plan was supposed to save the district money. However, many students lost stability in the process, and only time will tell the cost it will have on their lives.

That first town hall meeting was not just about consequences or the review of the schoolwide discipline system. It was also about the positive things that were being offered at Strawberry

Mansion as part of our turnaround model, all designed with the needs of the students in mind. During the town hall I explained the major components of the plan. I announced over and over again that Mansion was not a place where you came to do what you wanted. I told them that it was a place where you came to be educated. I mentioned that there would be gender-separate literature and algebra classes to cut down on the distractions in the two areas that needed attention the most. I outlined the honors program that would begin with ninth grade. To qualify, you simply had to be proficient in math and English on the PSSA. After careful review of the eighth-grade test scores, only 28 incoming eighth-graders qualified for the ninth-grade honors program. Out of the 28 expected proficient students assigned to Mansion, only three actually attended. Despite these alarming numbers, I was still committed to that honors program. If three students needed something different, I was prepared to give them something different. They were given the graduation requirements and an explanation of the core values (tradition, integrity, excellence, focus, and perseverance) that would be developed over the course of four years in order for them to pursue their dreams.

I then discussed the Alternative Education Program for the students who needed a shorter school day and additional credits in order to graduate. These students would be overage, and under-credited. They would be teenage mothers or fathers. They would be caregivers. Any students who fit into the high-risk category for dropping out of school, or any student in the community under 21 who wanted to come back to school, could enroll in the Alternative Education Program. We were willing to try anything traditional or non-traditional to help them to learn as much as they could in the time that we had them.

After the school discipline system and some components of the turnaround model were outlined, I wanted the students to know that school was supposed to be fun. I told them that in order for it to be fun, they had to take part in the activities that would be offered. Then, with much confidence, I stood tall and announced that next school year there would be football at Strawberry Mansion High School. That statement was not rehearsed. It was not part of my turnaround model on paper. It just came to me at the time, and I said it. That statement caused the teachers and the students to take pause, because Strawberry Mansion High School had never had a football team in its nearly 50-year history.

In August prior to opening, I had seen some young men walking down the street with football uniforms on. When I walked into Strawberry Mansion that morning, I asked the secretary and the building engineer when the Mansion football players would be reporting for preseason. They said in unison that Strawberry Mansion did not have a football team. I was startled and surprised by that. When I walked into my office, I called the athletic department at the school district, and they confirmed what the others had said. Strawberry Mansion had never had a football team. I was amazed and speechless. A high school in an area where sports are children's lifelines, and there was no football? Shortly after my football inquiry, I received a phone call from a friend of mine at one of the court-appointed disciplinary placement sites. My friend there said he was sending me a new student. He said that he was a great kid and an excellent football player who had just landed in some trouble. He then asked whether we had a football team, and I had to say "No." He was disappointed, because the student played ball at the disciplinary placement site and it had started to change his life. That phone call was confirmation for me that I had to get Strawberry Mansion a football team. I did not know how I was going to do it, but it was going to happen.

The students looked at me with disbelief, but I thought I could also see some hope in their eyes. One of the teachers later told me that he was interested in football, so it piqued his interest and caused him to wonder who I was, and how I was going to make football a reality at Mansion. Everyone left the town hall meeting on a positive note—not just focused on consequences, but also well-informed about the plan to make Strawberry Mansion a school. They no longer had to guess what was going to happen. They were told what was going to happen from me, the principal!

The "We do what we want" mentality did not immediately go away, of course. It was demonstrated numerous times during the first few weeks of school. Every one of the non-negotiable rules was broken before the first week was over. Despite the harsh consequence of an out-of-school suspension and the process for returning to school after the suspension was over, many of the same students continued to break the same rules over and over again. Fighting, propping the doors open to let people in and out, hall walking and refusing to go into the classroom, cursing at teachers—you name it, they did it. And every time they broke a non-negotiable rule, they had the same consequence: to spend time at home with their parents.

I know that the research says that schools should abolish zero tolerance regulations. Well, that is easy to say when critics of these laws do not have their own children in low-performing schools plagued with violence. What is a school to do when you have many adolescents refusing to follow any rules? For example, when the response to, "Young man, will you please go to class?" is, "Bitch, get out of my face. I am not moving and you cannot make me move"? What is a school to do when a student says "f--- you, this is our school and we do things our way"? What is a school to do when students blatantly defy every directive from teachers and support staff? Or when a large number of its students say, "We are not doing it, and we will run you out before we comply with your rules"? What are schools to do when 75 percent of the student body comes to school each day to learn and do the right thing, and the other 25 percent is making school a nightmare for them? Proponents of zero tolerance always talk about what principals should not do to the students who are compromising the safety and welfare of other students, but no one talks about what we should do for the students who come to school to learn and are forced to stay in deplorable, fearful conditions because somebody thinks zero tolerance is a bad idea. Suspension of the disruptive students gives the students who want to learn a chance to learn. It was my job to create an environment for them to learn, and I was not going to have them come to school in fear because another group of students refused to follow rules. Zero tolerance makes it possible to create an environment conducive to learning for all students and staff involved. If zero tolerance is only based on five rules, the students should know they must follow them. It is also the responsibility of the parents to insist that they do so, and that is what the parents are told when they bring them back to school.

I also know that many people argue that adolescents want to be suspended so they can stay home. By suspending them, we are giving them what they want. But that notion is far from the truth. Disruptive students have power in school, so that is where they want to be. No other consequence that I have found works to alter the behavior of disruptive students other than out-of-school suspensions, if they are done correctly. How do I know? I have tried many other alternatives: calling parents, detentions, in-school suspensions, prizes, rewards, tickets. . . . Nothing works with severely disruptive students because all of those options allow them to do one thing: enter the building. Once they are in the building, nothing else matters; power is what they seek.

Another area that needed a lot of attention was lunch period. Lunchroom duty was one of my most important assignments of the day. This was my time to get a pulse on the school and find out all the happenings. In addition, the school district was uncomfortable with my decision to go with one lunch period. Prior to my arrival, there were four lunch periods. Four lunch periods with 300 children was not going to happen. I heard horror stories of the way the students would behave in the lunchroom. The lunchroom was another place where they acted on the "We do what we want" theme. I was told that the students would stay in the lunchroom for all four lunch periods. They would enter the lunchroom at the sound of the bell, jump over the railing, and grab the food and run. They did this because they did not want anyone to see them eating the free lunch. They called the lunch "freebies," and that was something to be ashamed about; so they did not want to eat the food in front of other people. This process happened four times a day. I knew one 30-minute lunch period was the answer, and that order had to be implemented.

The doors leading in and out of the lunchroom were labeled with the letters A to E. Two officers were assigned to door D and E. Climate staff were assigned to doors A, B, and C. They had to stay on post at all times, unless a fight erupted in the lunchroom. The conflict resolution specialist, climate manager, one officer, and I circulated in the lunchroom. That gave me the opportunity to talk with the students about anything. It was my favorite part of the day. By talking to the students up close and building solid relationships with them, I got to know them and they got to know and understand what I was trying to do. Each time I spoke with them, I would call them by their last names and respond to them by calling them "Mr. ____" or "Miss _____." I wanted to show them a sign of respect so that they would show others the same. Showing respect goes a long way in building relationships. When I would start our conversation with Mr. or Miss, it would startle them and force them to listen. I had to get them to understand that I meant them no harm. All I had was love for them, and that is why I expected and demanded that they come to school, get an education, and learn to follow rules.

The lunchroom was very large—17,261 square feet, with 6,536 square feet designated for the preparation area. For the rest, I had to come up with a way to section it off, to make it appear smaller and manageable. Zones were created by putting the word "Zone" and a number on large poster paper on a pillar in each area. This created 10 zones. The tables were neatly arranged in each zone. A climate worker was assigned to monitor each zone. Students could sit anywhere; they weren't assigned to a particular zone. Through experience, I learned that adolescents are creatures of habit. If given the choice they would sit in the same zone every day, and they did. That is how I got to know their names,

their friends' names, and their enemies' names. By their position-
ing in the zones I could tell what was happening and what was
about to happen every minute in the lunchroom.

With a system in place for monitoring the lunchroom, a new
process for eating lunch was required. The students were to walk
into the lunchroom, take a seat in any zone, and wait until their
zone was called. Which zone went first was chosen randomly.
When their zone was called, students in that zone would walk
to the line and wait to be served, and then return to the zone
where they were sitting. There would be no running into the
lunchroom, jumping, and grabbing food. The cafeteria staff were
thankful for the new system. There would no longer be a reason
for them to stand back away from the food in fear of the students
getting out of control.

Each day during the first week of school, I arrived in the
lunchroom before the students entered and positioned myself in
the front of the lunchroom holding my bullhorn. As they arrived,
I yelled through the bullhorn "Have a seat, have a seat!" over and
over again. "If you do not come in and take a seat, lunch will not
be served." Everything was in place. I had assigned each climate
staff member a post. It was now time to call the zones for lunch.
"Zone 1, let's go." No one moved from his or her seats. "Zone
2, let's go." No one moved. "Zone 3, time for lunch. Let's go."
Much to my surprise, no one moved. Day after day, the students
entered the lunchroom and sat in their seats, but no one would
walk to the front of the lunchroom to get lunch. They just sat
there in their zones, talking and ignoring my call to get up and
get their lunches. I had never seen anything like that before.
How were they being so controlled, so disciplined not to get up
and eat, even though they might be hungry? I tried to coax them
to get their lunch by saying "Come on! Come on." They would
not get out of their seats, no matter what I said to them. It was a
standoff each day. Power was what they wanted, at all costs.

At one point, students started shouting, "We do not want
those freebies, freebies, freebies." I looked over at my conflict
resolution specialist and my climate manager in disbelief. You

could see that many of the students wanted to get up to eat, but would not out of fear. After a week of this standoff, the cafeteria workers grew concerned about all of the wasted food they had to throw away each day. With each passing day of rebellion, I wanted to give up on my process, even though I knew it was the right thing to do to maintain order and safety. But I did not want the students who needed the food to go home hungry. Just when I was about to let them get up freely and get lunch like the old days, I decided to yell through the bullhorn, and give it one more attempt. In a loud, but humbled voice I said, "So, how long are you going to keep this up? How long are you going to go home hungry? Really? *Really?* All because I want you to eat in an orderly fashion and understand that there is no shame in eating a free school lunch, you are going to go home hungry? This makes no sense!" The lunchroom was silent. I finally had all of their attention. Then, just when I was about to put the bullhorn down and say just go ahead and eat, a student stood up and slowly walked from the back of the lunchroom to the front. "Mrs. Wayman," he said, "you are right. You people are crazy. I am getting my lunch." He was seen as a leader in the building at the time. If he said do it, they all did it, and that is just what happened. After he got in line, he instructed me to call the zones and they all got in line. That was the end of the standoff. I was so happy, I wanted to cry. This was also the day that I started singing "Happy Birthday" to my students, even though I cannot hold a tune. I had won that round publicly, but not in my heart. That day was another sign that this principalship would be like no other. I had to be prepared to go the distance, even if it made me feel uncomfortable. If Strawberry Mansion High School was going to be a safe school, I had to erase that "We do what we want" mindset from my students' minds. But what I also discovered on this day was that singing "Happy Birthday" went a long way in building relationships.

My team put countless hours into designing a turnaround model to make Strawberry Mansion High School a school. We were well versed in the issues our students faced, and we were willing to address all of their needs, but we were not going to allow them to deter us from our major task—and that was to educate them. They tried every way they could think of to retain the power they had before my team arrived: We made a rule, they broke the rule. We created a system, they undermined the system. We dreamed, they doubted. But through it all, we stayed steadfast to our vision for the school. At times we were shaken, but overjoyed when the structure held firm.

My "word" and my "actions" were being tested. I know that happens before real change happens, so I welcome defiance. I also know that, as a leader, my word and my actions make change possible. I say what I mean and I do what I say, at all costs, even when it is risky to do so.

## Thinking About Your Leadership

As a leader your words and your actions are tested every minute. Never say anything you cannot take action on. Remember that everyone remembers your words and your actions. When you do not keep your word and do not take action when necessary, it will destroy your turnaround efforts.

**Examine Attentively:** Your words and your actions.

**Questions for You:**

- Do you keep your word? Do you do what you say you are going to do?
- Are you steadfast? Do you take action when you need to take action or do you let things go?

# 18

# Realize

Over the first two months, the school continued to experience many challenges. One group of students who had a stronghold on the other was determined to keep their power, so they continued to break the rules. But breaking non-negotiable rules landed them at home. The suspensions were racking up, but order was in sight.

Many questions preyed on my mind. Why are the students so defiant? Why won't they just follow simple rules? Why don't their parents insist they follow the rules? Why do their parents fight us for insisting their children follow the rules? Why are some of the students so mean with their words and actions? Why are they so disrespectful to the teachers and the staff? The questions just kept coming. How was I going to make Strawberry Mansion a school? How was I supposed to protect all of the students and staff without turning the school into a prison? What could be done to decrease the suspensions among the same 25 percent of the student population without jeopardizing the entire schoolwide behavior system? There were so many things to attend to that my mind never rested. I was always on edge, waiting for the next storm to arrive. I could feel the unrest. That is how in tune I had to become to mentally prepare for what was to come. Questioning kept me aware and alert.

Resistance from the students to keep Strawberry Mansion High School like it was before my arrival was fast and furious.

Fear was an everyday occurrence. The burden of making sure everyone got home safely was at times almost too much to bear. There were days when I told God I was not going to make it. Especially after a student told me to my face that I needed a "motherfuckin bullet in my head." I could not believe what I had heard. I stood there and tried to process why he would say such a thing to me. I was just asking him to leave the building after school hours. After he said those words, he ran out of the building. I wondered whether he was going to get a gun to shoot me. Did he have a gun outside? Was he going to wait for me and shoot me on the way to my car? I went back to my office and called my Philadelphia police officer. He asked me the student's name and said he would call it in. It was long past 3:00 p.m. when I left for the evening, and all I could think of as I walked to my car was that someone who told me I needed a bullet in my head was out there somewhere, waiting for me. All the students talked about in the lunchroom was guns. I knew that if he wanted to kill me, he could. Guns are everywhere in this neighborhood. I hurried to my car looking around for him or anyone else parked in a car or standing nearby who could cause me harm. I locked my doors and drove off, relieved and thinking of nothing except my two daughters. I thought about my children motherless, and burst into tears. My funeral actually flashed before me. Did he really hate me that much for trying to create order in a school so that he and others could learn? My God, what was going on in here?

When I arrived home I made a promise to never tell my family, especially my two daughters, what was said to me. I didn't want them to worry, and they were already questioning my decision to go to Strawberry Mansion. I would answer their questions by saying that it was my assignment. They never understood that answer, but I kept saying it anyway. I was their mother. They just wanted me out of there, but that was not about to happen. I feared the guns. Every day I asked God to protect my students and my staff, and to please send me home at night to my children.

Daily announcements were the time for me to discuss everything with my students and staff at once. They happened every morning at the same time, and each time it started with me yelling into the public address system to get their undivided attention:

Good morning! Good morning! Strawberry Mansion students and staff, good morning! Here is your announcement for today.

Young people, I am still waiting for my petitions to be signed so that we can present the signatures to the school district to ask for our football team. I want as many signatures as possible from the community. I need you to take the petitions to everyone. Here is your incentive: the two people who collect the highest number of signatures will get a gift card from me. No, I am not telling you the amount. I need the signatures, and I need them by Friday. I will then present them to the district and get us a football team. Okay, okay . . . I need your help. . . .

Please make sure you remember to follow the non-negotiable rules. They are important, and they are non-negotiable. Advisors, please remember to go over the rules daily with your students. And this is a reminder that we are having our monthly town hall assembly program this morning. Soon, I will ask for all of you to come to the auditorium with your teachers. Each month we must get better and better with how to behave in the auditorium. Teachers, when I call you, please bring your students to the auditorium. Thank you. And remember—if nobody told you they loved you today, remember I do, and I always will.

Today we were scheduled to have a nonviolence assembly. The Department of Justice sponsored the program. As the students filed into the auditorium, the representative was expressing his enthusiasm for the presentation that was about to be shown. "Mrs. Wayman, it is great! We had a lot of success last year in schools similar to this one." I made it known in our previous meetings that I was not crazy about the idea of having a nonviolence assembly, for several reasons. Nevertheless, I had promised him in the summer that I would allow this assembly as part of the help I was receiving from the U.S. Attorney's office.

As the students were filing into the auditorium, I was being briefed on the first day of youth court. That was an additional program sponsored by the Department of Justice to help cut down on out-of-school suspensions. Youth court allowed their peers to decide what infraction they should receive for breaking other rules besides the five non-negotiable rules. Community service was given for these infractions.

The students were filing into the auditorium in an unorganized fashion. They just were not used to coming to the auditorium on a regular basis. It took several minutes to get them settled. I needed the bullhorn siren to get that to happen. They did not like the siren because it made a really loud noise and it startled them. When it was finally quiet, the first presenter came to the stage. He was from the Philadelphia Eagles. He was included in the program because we thought that it would be exciting for them to meet a real Eagle, but they did not treat him very well. Of course it didn't help that the team was coming off of a losing season, but the students had absolutely no respect for the position. They booed him right off the stage. I knew right then that this was going to be a long morning.

The presenter of the nonviolence program began with a story about his brother being bullied in school that lead to some bad choices on his part. He went on to say that this was a nonviolence assembly program aimed to prevent bullying. Part of the program involved watching a film. I knew nothing about the program (which was an error on my part), so I did not know what to expect. I got a little nervous when they had to watch a film because that meant I had to bring the lights down. I circulated the room, worried, but not enough to end it. The film started to play. The teachers seemed a little nervous as well. It was only our third assembly program, and the students' behavior was less than desirable. The teachers were just trying to keep the students calm. They were not focused on anything else.

As the movie began to play, I was surprised that it was some sort of reenactment of the Columbine High School shooting. I was growing more and more concerned, because I did not know how this program was going to teach nonviolence after showing violence. Then I remembered that bullying played a large part in the Columbine tragedy. My heart started to beat very fast, and I was scared. I kept telling myself to turn the lights on and end it, but I did not want to be rude; and I also needed the partnership with the Department of Justice. Having them involved with the school gave me some sense of security. I had to believe that this program had some substance.

The longer they watched the video, the louder they got. At first I did not know whether it was groans of anger or fear from what they were watching. Much to my surprise, it was not groans I was hearing. Instead, it was uncontrollable laughter. But if they were watching something so mean and devastating, why were they laughing? What was so funny? The presenter and I looked at each other, stunned by their response. Why were they laughing at the sight of something so horrific?

My teachers were in sheer panic. Finally, the film ended with some kind of message, but I do not remember what it was. I was fixated on the students, who continued to laugh uncontrollably after viewing one of the worst things I have ever seen. After seeing that reaction, the presenter and I were so shaken that we had to understand why the students reacted in that manner at something so tragic. We decided to bring a group of the ninth-graders together for a roundtable discussion. After we entered a large classroom next to the auditorium, I asked the first question. "Can someone please tell me what was so funny about that video? It was not meant to be funny." One of my three honor students said in a very serious and downtrodden tone, "Mrs. Wayman, you think that is really something, but that is nothing compared to what we see on the streets each night. We see a whole lot worse than that every day when we go home." I sat back in the chair and thought they were not being mean, they were just numb from their own trauma. The laughter was their internal pain releasing itself. While they were talking in this discussion group, they were just so sad and depressed. Every word they spoke led to a spirit of hopelessness.

The three adults left that session more somber than the students. We felt their pain, and the pain from the Columbine incident. It was a very sad day for the people who had come to help me. It was a devastating day for me. I felt defeated in that moment. But I also knew that was a defining moment for how I would lead Strawberry Mansion High School. My students were in pain. Deep pain from all of the ills of the world placed upon them. Every injustice in the world converged on the steps of Strawberry Mansion High School. Homelessness, poverty, incarceration, absent or deceased parents, schools that weren't schools . . . what a mess. I learned a lot that day in November, but my biggest lesson was the deep despair my students were living with from day to day. Their defiant, disrespectful "I do what I want" and "I do not care" attitude was directly related to their circumstances. When they would say, "I don't care," they really meant it. They believed that nothing was going to change in their world, and their world was all they knew. Bullying, violence, trauma, and tragedy ruled their world. That is why they were full of despair. To make matters worse, students who were full of hope were forced to merge with children who had no hope, and that hopelessness prevailed in all of them. That is why Strawberry Mansion was different from any school I had encountered in my 30-year career. I had never encountered children who really believed they were worthless. There was nobody to care or to intervene on their behalf, so all of the students were just mad, angry, complacent, and numb. That is why they always said "Whatever" when being spoken to. On that day, November 19, 2012, I got it. That assembly was for me to learn something, not the students. That day, I knew I had to stay the course that I had already laid out, but I also had to find avenues to give hope to the hopeless.

At the end of the day, I sat in my blue leadership chair, still numb from my discovery—but already thinking about next steps. Strawberry Mansion was forcing me to think outside the box from every angle just to get the students out of their state of despair. I had to be open to looking at the vision in a more complex way to add a new approach to my design for change. Yes, making Strawberry Mansion a school was the goal. But in order for that to happen, I had to pour patience, flexibility, experience, expectations, and a whole lot of love into that school in order to build trust and give my students a reason to fight for their lives.

## Thinking About Your Leadership

Sometimes when you set out to lead with your well-developed action plan, something arises to expose the underlying problems in the organization. When this happens, pause to say "ah-ha," and change the course of action to address those problems immediately. Realizing and addressing the underlining problems gives you a greater chance at success. If you do not address them, your mission will surely fail.

**Examine Attentively:** The signals to expand your course of corrective action.

**Questions for You:**

- What evidence do you have that signals the need to expand your course of action?
- How will you recognize and address the underlying problems in your organization?

# 19

# Confidence

In the weeks that followed the assembly, I was committed to trying to find ways to inspire hope in my students. There were supposed to be follow-up sessions to the program, but I postponed them all until I could get a handle on the students' state of mind. I asked my secretary to arrange as many trips as possible outside of the community. She managed to book one or two outings a month to colleges, cultural centers, and team-building events. I was trying to get them to see something different outside of the neighborhood, as my mom had done for me, to give them an image of what to strive for. I wanted them to see that there was an entire world out there far beyond their despair. I wanted them to know that education was the first step to overcome all of the mean things that had happened to them. I wanted them to focus on what could be, instead of what was. I wanted them to see the beauty of the world and recognize the place they could have in it. There was no prescription for instilling hope. I knew that leaving the neighborhood on those long bus rides with my mom gave me hope while living in poverty, and I prayed that the trips we planned would to the same for them.

Being poor limits your options to everyday activities most take for granted. Going to the movies, the zoo, skating, and on vacations were all things you may have done a few times in childhood if you were lucky. My mom became very creative about exposing my two sisters and me to the beautiful things in life outside of our North Philadelphia community, and at the same time, filled the time with her own designed activities for us. Riding the bus on Sundays used to be free for children, so mom took advantage of that. Some Sundays after church, we would ride different bus routes from the beginning of the route to the end of the route. All along the way, my mom would point out things that she wanted us to have. She would say, "Look Linda, do you like that house? If you want that house you have to go to school. Do you like that car? You have to go to school if you want that car." Then my sisters and I would try to look for the best house on the street and claim that we would own it someday. That made my mother smile. Those bus trips were her way to spend time with us and show us what a good education could provide for us. The exposure was what she was after in order to have us dream. It was the strategy that I would now use to provide my students with hope.

I knew that winning something would also go a long way in providing hope—especially, winning against an establishment like the school district. There were so many naysayers. I was told that it was impossible to get a football team at Strawberry Mansion. I heard things like "You all have not had a football team in nearly 50 years, why would they give it to you now?" A win I thought would definitely give the student population another reason to be hopeful. And any instance of hope would make a difference.

The days ahead were tough. The girls had major conflicts daily. Fighting among the girls happened in school, on the way to school, and on the way home from school. All they did was fight. They were suspended every time. I was so worried about the fighting that I had to ban the girls from wearing scarves on their heads to school. Not religious head coverings, just scarves tied on their heads to cover their hair. For the most part, it represented that a fight was going to happen. I was trying to tackle fear and hope all at the same time.

One beautiful fall morning at 8:00 a.m., three girls who were normally late arrived to school on time. Their hair was covered with beautiful scarves, and the handsome young man who usually rounded out their foursome was missing. Ms. Jackson was standing at the door as they approached the body-scan machine, and told them that they had to take off their scarves. One of the girls, who never spoke to anyone, even when spoken to, said "Good morning" in a happy voice. Ms. Jackson was startled, because she never spoke to anyone. She wondered why they were without the boy they were usually with, but didn't ask. Ms. Jackson really loved two of the three girls because they were always together, and were often glared at because of their large size. So when they told her the sob story that they knew the rule about the scarves but that their hair had to be combed before they could go to class, she believed them and told them to hurry up and go to the bathroom, take off the scarves, comb their hair, and get to class. Three minutes had not passed before one of the climate staff started screaming over the walkie-talkie. "Code one! Oh my God, code one!" That was the code given for a major assault.

The three girls had barged into a classroom and started assaulting a student. Apparently something had happened in the neighborhood the night before, and the girls were retaliating. Ms. Jackson was upset with herself for not staying focused on the rules, and the girls were so upset that they did not tell Ms. Jackson what was going on and instead took matters into their own hands. After that incident, neither the three girls nor the girl who had been assaulted returned to Mansion. We found out later that the boy who was not with the three girls the day of the assault had been standing on a nearby corner and was shot in the chest; luckily, the shot was not fatal. He was able to return to school briefly, but the fear of remaining in the same neighborhood as the shooting was too much to bear, so he transferred out of the area. Fear was something that was real in school, and on the way to and from school. Instilling hope would not be easy.

The staff worked on appropriate ways to handle daily conflict. Conflict happened so often that we had to increase our staff from one conflict resolution specialist to two. The students were just angry about everything. Minute things would escalate into huge disputes, which often turned violent. A lot of mediation sessions had to take place to keep all situations under control. Everyone was on constant alert. I told the teachers to listen to the students' conversations carefully. If there was an argument, even just a small controversy, I instructed them to call the office for support right away before it turned into something we couldn't handle. I told the teachers that the students normally argued and yelled at each other before they threw one punch, so to please call the office before any argument turned into an act of violence.

It was our daily mission to keep fear under control, and hope very much alive. The students needed guidance, structure, a framework for success, something to believe in, and much patience and love every day. This was our formula to increase the chances for our students to escape poverty and become successful adults.

School announcements over the public address system were in large pep talks with a purpose for the students and staff, and a typical announcement went like this:

> Good afternoon, everyone. Before you go home today, I want to tell you that we have two winners for the petition drive. We have collected over 800 signatures to present to the district to get our football team. We are going to get a team for next school year! I will let you know the next step after I turn the petitions over to the district. Also, I want you to bring in your five dollars to go on the college trip next week. Remember, we have to pay for the bus. I want the bus full, so bring your five dollars. Young people, I want you to remember that education can save your life. I want you to follow the rules, listen to your teachers, and do your work so that you can graduate from high school. Be safe going home, and remember—if nobody told you they loved you today, remember I do, and I always will.
>
> Oh, and do not forget that we have a young men's varsity basketball game today. It is free, and all are welcome. I said *free*. There will be no fundraiser today.

Making the game free of charge would increase the chances they would attend, and stay off the streets a little while longer.

Those daily announcements were my way of keeping the lines of communication open with the students and staff. I was always honest with those announcements. Some of the things

I said could be seen as controversial, but I always knew what I had to say to get their attention; instilling hope was what I was after.

The basketball game I announced that time was a great one. It was the first time that we had gathered without any conflict. The coach wanted the game closed to the students and the community because he was concerned about the violence. I listened, and then closed it to the community, but not to the student body. Every student who wanted to attend was permitted to attend. The game was very crowded. The students gathered with a common goal: to win against another team. It was the first time in public that we were one school. No one shouted "We are from Fitzsimons" or "We are from Rhodes." We were Strawberry Mansion High School as we cheered together for our team to win; and they did win. At the end of the game, we were so excited, and there were smiles all around. Strawberry Mansion High School had won a basketball game we were predicted to lose. Everyone filed out of the gym beaming with pride. It felt so good. The smiles on their faces were priceless, and that made me so happy. I walked the students to the door to exit the school. We hugged each other in our excitement over the victory.

After the last student gave me a hug, and before I could close the door completely behind her, she quickly retreated back into the school. "Mrs. Wayman," she said, "there are news cameras out there." I asked her to go over to the news reporter and ask why they were in front of the school filming. She did as I directed her to do, then ran back into the building and said, "Oh my God, Mrs. Wayman, they said we are closing. They said that Strawberry Mansion High School is on the school closure list. We are set to close at the end of the school year." She hugged me again and I told her to go home. After she left I felt so sick I could barely make it back to my office. I was aware that the school closure list was set for release, but I was not concerned. When I was assistant superintendent, I was in the conversation about which schools might close, and Strawberry Mansion was never on the list. How and why did Strawberry Mansion get on the school closure list, and without anyone from central office warning me? I reached my office and sat in my blue leadership chair. My God, I thought, how much pain can be afflicted onto the same set of students? How could people who were supposed to love children be so cruel? These children had nothing, absolutely nothing left to give. And now, they even wanted to take away the school building—when I was doing everything I could to make that building function as a source of hope.

I checked my email and there it was, the invitation to attend a meeting the next morning for all of the schools up for closure. There it was in black and white. The school closure list included Strawberry Mansion High School. The date is forever etched in my mind: December 12, 2012. The rug had just been pulled from under me. I was numb. To make matters worse, I found out the school I was leading was up for closure from news reporters. I wished I could have at least prepared my children, but once again, they found out something in a very traumatic way on the one day they were actually happy.

I reported for work the next morning in a somber mood, but I suppressed it the moment I entered the building. The staff were very upset. The students were worried. Their faces showed their horror at the thought of being moved to another school. I was determined to be the optimist. I sent a response email to my former executive assistant that said: "They think we are closing, but we are not." I kept telling everyone not to worry, because we were not going to close without putting up a fight. I did not know what the fight would look like, but I was confident that I was not going to go down without a fight. The last conversation I had with the former superintendent came to mind. She told me that if I loved children as I claimed, I would have to come work at central office because the day would come that I would need that experience to continue to work on behalf of poor children. This was that day.

I could not stop wondering how Strawberry Mansion managed to get on the school closure list. The email outlined the time and place of an emergency school closure meeting with the school district officials and the affected school principals. Thirty-seven schools were up for closure in some capacity, so all 37 principals were expected to be at the meeting at 10:00 a.m. The email said to be on time, even though it was a difficult time. It also said,

"We will need the support of the principals to make this process as smooth as possible."

After I read the email, I immediately made plans for my absence. I announced to my entire office staff, "Today, when I get to the meeting, I am not going to say a word." They all looked at me in surprise because I was always outspoken and I had just told them we were not going to close without a fight. The truth is that I was too afraid that my anger could not be controlled, so silence was the only way for me to guarantee that I would not be unprofessional. It would be the first time meeting with the new superintendent, who had arrived in Philadelphia in July 2012.

As I was about to leave the office, my roster chairman handed me a document from the Neighborhood Crime Statistics section of the Philadelphia Police Department website. He was searching for anything that could possibly make the argument to keep the school open. The document contained statistical data about the crime rate in the Strawberry Mansion area. It outlined the murder rate of young African American men who were school age and should have been enrolled in Mansion. The many black dots represented dead teenagers. I placed the paper in my pocketbook and left for the meeting.

When I walked into the auditorium at 440 North Broad Street, there were 37 sad principals seated in rows. No one was talking to anyone else. We all sat there as if we were just struck by lightning. The school officials came in from a side entrance and lined up across the front of the room. The superintendent was among them, along with the young woman responsible for collecting data that informed the process. The program began with questions. One of the officials had a microphone, which she handed to principal after principal. Through it all, I did not make a sound. My face was like stone, showing no emotion. I was desperately trying to keep myself calm. I coached myself not to say anything. It seemed like several principals were asking the same question because the school district officials were not able to answer any of their questions. This question dodging went on and on, but I kept holding my tongue, even though by this point I wanted to scream. Finally, another principal got up and asked the same question the principal before her had asked, and got the same dodging of the answer the other principals received. This time, I lost it. When the principal went to return the microphone to the school district official, I put my hand out and took the microphone and stood up as she asked if there were any more questions. I then yelled *"This is unconscionable! What is wrong with you people? This is unconscionable!"* I looked at the superintendent and his staff and asked,

> "Do you know what you are doing? How in the world did Strawberry Mansion get on a closure list? Are you aware that the students I have now are coming from a closure last school year? So you are going to move them *again*? How can you all sleep at night?" I then reached down and grabbed the data sheet from my pocketbook and held it up. I yelled, "Do you see this? Do you see the dots? The dots represent the dead bodies of children who are school age and belong to Mansion. If you close this school, where are they going to go? You have closed all the schools in the neighborhood, and the charter schools will not take my children. Where are they going to go to school?"

> I then turned my attention to the other 36 principals in the room.

> "When they closed Rhodes and Fitzsimons and I asked you to take my children, some of you would not take them. You did not want them. So where are you going to send my children if you close the school?" Then I singled out one of the school officials and pointed my finger and said, "How could you? How could you? You know you are wrong. You promised my Rhodes girls that Strawberry Mansion would be a better option. That was not the reality. Now you want to close Mansion. . ."

The official I was directing my anger at became so upset that she left the room crying. Every principal in the room was now crying because they felt the same pain I was feeling, but could not bring themselves to articulate it. We were all on the list for various reasons. Even though there was no clear reason for why Mansion was added to the list, it did not matter. We were all one in our pain. Data cannot reflect the connection that a principal has for a school. That cannot be measured in any data set. I, too, began to cry like all of my fellow principals, and took a seat. The superintendent grabbed the microphone and adjourned the meeting, even though it was supposed to go on for two more hours. It was just too emotional for all of us. It had to end.

I was right back to where I had started in July, trying to convince everyone that my children deserved a great school. *Yes*, they had a lot of challenges and misplaced anger, but adults in their lives caused that pain; and now, to put extra salt in the wound, the school system had decided that their education could be interrupted time and time again. How could these children not be angry? Everywhere they turned there was an obstacle, but being educated should not have been one of them. It is a right afforded to them by being a citizen of the United States of America, and it was my job to make sure everybody lived up to that creed. To make sure this happened, I was charged with tackling hope and fear in various ways at the same time; and I was confident in the end that hope and the sense for what was right would prevail.

## Thinking About Your Leadership

Hope is the belief that something can change for the better. For without it all, efforts are a waste of time. Go into your turnaround challenge with the expectation that you are the one who will bring consistent hope to the situation, and spend some time instilling it in others. Always be positive about how the challenge will turn out. Confident turnaround leaders make hope their driving force.

**Examine Attentively:** Your expectations as the keeper of hope for your organization. Spread it often!

**Questions for You:**
- Are you hopeful? Do you really believe everything will turn out in your favor? Do you spread that hope among your staff?
- Are you prepared to stand up against the status quo to lead your vision to reality?

# 20

# Influence

I went back to work after the school closure meeting. I was overwhelmed by the gathering, and tired of hearing the word "closure." I sat at my desk in my blue leadership chair trying to figure out what do next. The meeting ended with district officials asking for principal support to go through the closure process. To me, that just meant: "Do not get in the district's way. Just show up and do what you are asked to do." That was not going to happen. I had to find a way to avoid afflicting more trauma on my students. Of course I had a family and cared about my job, but I could not let that stop me from doing what was right for the students at Strawberry Mansion High School.

I knew I was going to do whatever I could to keep Mansion open, with every ounce of strength I had left. The fight was not just for what was happening now, but also for what had happened to me and all of the other children in the area for years. The same community had endured experiment after experiment: desegregation; a racial imbalance of teachers; a rotating door of administrators and teachers, educational management companies, charters, and closures. No wonder the incarceration rate was so high in the neighborhood that surrounding this community. Yes, many would argue that if the school or schools in the North Philadelphia area are so terrible, just close them. However, it is not that simple. If you close schools and do not give students the opportunity to attend a better school, this just adds to the dysfunction of an already dysfunctional community. High schools are the beacon of the community, whether they are perceived as good or bad. Instead of closing a school, fix the school by giving it the structure and support it needs. Strong leadership, teachers, and staff are the foundation for any great school.

Prior to the threat of closure, I met a woman who lived in the neighborhood. She was a very concerned citizen who came into the school one day to report an incident she had witnessed in the community. The Philadelphia police officer assigned to the school walked into my office while she was giving her statement. She became silent. She said, "I do not talk in front of cops. That is not safe in this neighborhood." I remembered her because she had a lot of spirit and really cared for the neighborhood. She was the first person I thought about when I realized I would need community support to keep Mansion open. I contacted her. She was very eager to help in any way she could, and she contacted a young man to assist us both. The three of us met on a regular basis to work on how to save Strawberry Mansion from closure. They were both well-connected in the community and involved in local politics. They were respected in the neighborhood, and they could use their clout to draw on the community to come to a meeting to strategize on how to stop the closure. They could handle everything.

The two community leaders drew a large crowd for each of our strategy sessions. They were very heated meetings. Everyone expressed their anger one at a time at the possible closing of Strawberry Mansion High School, even though many of their children did not attend the school. The community viewed it as the taking of one more thing from them, and they were not going to have it. They were willing to do anything to keep the school open. One of the community leaders addressed the crowd very eloquently. She told them that her grandson went to the school next door, and wanted to come to Mansion. She asked everyone for his or her support to fight to keep Mansion open, and they agreed to help. As I stood in the shadows during the meeting to take it all in, I was impressed by the community's determination. The residents had had enough. They were not going to lose Strawberry Mansion High School. Many of the older residents stood up and gave the history of the school and how it almost was not built. The racist practices to prohibit African American contractors to assist in building the school halted production. They fought the establishment to be included, and they won. African American contractors helped to build Strawberry Mansion, and it would take the same community to save it.

At the meeting it was decided that the first line of business was to write letters to all of the city leaders: the mayor, city council members, the superintendent, and anyone else who could help keep the school open. Of course we contacted the Department of Justice to get support. Representatives made appointments with the superintendent on our behalf. We were going to fight to keep this school open, even though many people wondered why. The answer was simple: it was our building, and it was our intention to continue what we had started to make it a great school. We had two more meetings with the community after that night to prepare for our school closure meeting with district officials. It was the school's time to make the case for why the school should remain open. Our plan for the community meeting was simple: to fill every seat in our large auditorium that could seat more than 800 people The North Philadelphia community is known for their lack of participation in community affairs, so I asked the community leaders to go out with the simple but complex task to make sure every seat at the community meeting was filled.

As the meeting date loomed, the students were starting to comply more and more with the non-negotiable school rules. Suspensions were down, outside experiences were up, and the school year was moving along. Besides the daily "student compliance" battle, the battle to have a football team, and the school closure battle, there were two other major battles underway: teacher and support staff effectiveness, and the cold.

Getting the teachers and staff used to their roles in our effort to make Mansion a school was difficult. There was a lot for the teachers to get used to: new classroom spaces, a full load of classes, gender-separate classes, submitting weekly lesson plans for review, responding to principal feedback, tracking student progress, using a prescribed instructional format, emphasizing small group instruction, daily informal observations with feedback, and compliance with the schoolwide behavior system. Teachers were forbidden to give work packets in place of daily student attendance. The students were now out of the halls and in the classroom, but due to the massive amount of professional development needed for the teachers to teach to standards, the teachers struggled with giving the students grade-appropriate work. They had low expectations for what the students could do, and their knowledge for how to teach to standards was lacking. The teachers were just not used to the students being present in the classroom and having their instructional program monitored.

The support staff also had to be closely monitored for compliance with their outlined duties. They had to be reminded not to eat or sleep while on hall duty, to stay at their assigned posts, and not to use their cell phones except in extreme emergencies. There were people and cameras located in every hot spot. We needed each of them to monitor his or her area flawlessly, forming a safety net around everyone. The support staff had to be courageous. They were responsible for holding the entire safety system together, and they took the brunt of the anger from the students. The students were aware that if they could get the support staff to go against enforcing the non-negotiable behavior system, everything would fall apart. The support staff had to be comfortable with hallway ownership. They had the authority to place any students who belonged in a classroom on their floor back into the classroom. The teachers were told that they could not put any student into the hallway without a pass. If they did, he or she would be returned by the support staff. The teachers owned the classroom, and the support staff owned the hallways. This was a strategy used to build accountability between the two groups responsible for making the school a school.

Then there was the cold. Yes, the freezing cold. The students wanted to wear coats, hats, and hoodies in the classroom, but we were concerned that it would cause security concerns. And it was not normal for students to sit in classrooms with coats on and buttoned up because there was no heat in a school. We were desperately trying to get the students to use lockers (something they had not done in years), and the cold temperature in the building was making that impossible. After demanding that the heating be repaired by making excessive phone calls and direct emails to central office, the cold became less of a problem. Without the cold, the students could put their coats and other clothing in the lockers, after a lot of extensive conversations with them about why they should do so.

Our school reorganization meeting (a fancy name for a closure meeting!) was originally scheduled to be held on February 11th at Strawberry Mansion High School. Without warning, it was moved to January 8th and switched to another school across town. That was out of the ordinary. Why had the date, time, and location suddenly changed? This did not happen to any other school up for closure. How were my parents and community supporters going to go across town to the school closure meeting? We didn't know who was behind the changes, but it made us suspicious. The community worked tirelessly to get members of the community involved with the closure meeting. Since the district switched the location of the meeting out of our school, getting as many people as possible over to the new site of the meeting was going to be a challenge. We had heard rumors from other closure meeting attendees that district officials had not faced packed audiences. So when it was time for our meeting, now at Dobbins High School, they were not worried because it was widely anticipated that North Philadelphia residents would not come out in record numbers, especially if they had to travel across town. To change that narrative, my secretary created flyers, and the community leaders went door-to-door to put out the word about the meeting. Every time we were asked what someone could do to show support, we would tell them to show up at Dobbins. When asked what their role would be at Dobbins, we would say, "To sit in the chair." It became a running joke: "Please come to sit in the chair." Local businesses paid for buses to get neighborhood support over to Dobbins High School. We were serious about saving our school, and we prepared to have a successful meeting.

When the school district officials arrived for the meeting, you could see by the look of surprise on their faces that they never expected to see so many people in attendance. It was a magnificent turnout. I was so proud of the effort the community members gave to get so many people in attendance.

But there was a problem. Strawberry Mansion High School was located in the Dr. Ruth Wright Hare Educational complex, which also housed L.P. Hill Elementary School, and both schools in the complex were up for closure. We put our stop the closure efforts together, but now district officials wanted to split us up into two separate meetings.

The residents were already sitting down when it was announced that they should split up and go to different rooms based on which school they were there for. Nobody knew what to do, so I told the community leaders to tell everyone not to move. We would not split. That became the chant in the room: "We will not split. We are one. We are one. We are one." We grew concerned that divide and conquer was the strategy. We were not having any of that on this day.

The room continued to fill with more and more people, until it was standing room only. The noise level kept increasing, and you could feel the tension in the air. The school district officials took their places in the front of the auditorium, and the noise grew even louder. The district officials called for silence, trying to gain control of the room, but the noise only continued to grow. One of the district officials walked over to me and said, "If we do not gain control of the crowd, we are going to leave." Panic overcame me. All I could think of was that a mass riot would break out if they walked out of that room. I could not let that happen. We had worked too hard to put together a meeting by the community, and for the community, for them to walk out without hearing our concerns about the closure.

I quickly stood up, took the microphone from her, and said loudly to the crowd, "Excuse me, everyone! Are we really going to let them walk out of here and lose our opportunity to tell our stories for why our schools should stay open? Really? Are we going to allow that to happen?" It got a little quieter. "The children have something to say," I continued. "They are standing in line ready to take the microphone. We have to listen to our children. So please, let's quiet down so we can hear them. If you would like to speak, please step into the line so that you can have your turn to speak, but please be courteous so that they do not walk out." I then handed the microphone back to the moderator of the meeting. They were surprised at the reaction to my address to the crowd. I was willing to do anything within my power to control the situation so that they would not walk out of that room. I desperately wanted everyone to be heard. We needed to be heard!

Speaker after speaker stepped to the microphone to tell the story about why Mansion should stay open. One parent talked about her son who was in prison, and she outlined all of the failed district initiatives, or lack of initiatives, in his schools that had led to him becoming uneducated and incarcerated. A teacher stepped up and repeated the same story we had been recounting for a long time: that the same students would have encountered three different schools in three years if Mansion were to close. "Would you want your child in three different high schools in three years?" they asked. Next to speak was the student from Mansion who had been the first to eat lunch, ending the lunchtime revolt of the first few weeks of school. He said in a tender voice, "We love our school. We want it to get better, and it *is* getting better, but you keep changing the focus without giving us time to improve."

The line for speakers went on forever. Teachers, parents, students, and community folks all stepped up to the microphone to express their concerns. The meeting was supposed to end at 8:00 p.m. When that time arrived and a district official got in line to cut off the additional speakers, the participants in the room went crazy. "No! No! I want my turn. I WANT my TURN!" The superintendent went off his own script and allowed the comments to go well past the 8:00 p.m. deadline. He answered every question, and listened to every statement. The comments were hard to listen to. It was the same theme over and over: "Why our kids? Why keep experimenting with and taking from our children?"

The meeting ended late. Everyone filed out exhausted, but proud that we had had our say. Proud that the community came together with a common goal to save our school.

## Thinking About Your Leadership

When you are the leader you have influence. You must use your influence to get others to do the right thing for your organization and you must use that influence to make your community a better place to live. Leaders must use their influence without hesitation when it is needed to make a mission successful. Using influence responsibly is a major function of a leader.

**Examine Attentively:** Your ability to use your influence to make important change happen in your organization or in your community.

**Questions for You:**

- When your organization or community needs a voice, do you use your influence to make sure it is heard?
- Do you use your influence to make sure no barriers get in the way of the success of the mission?

# 21

# Possible

The morning after the school reorganization meeting, I arrived at work exhausted. I immediately fell into my blue leadership chair and felt a deep sense of pride. Proud that the community I loved had finally taken a stand on a very important issue: school closures. The outcome of the school closure decision mattered, and I was gratified that the community had taken a stand to prevent a wrong before it happened, instead of complaining about it after it happened, as was so often the case.

My announcement that morning was especially upbeat:

Good morning! Good morning, Strawberry Mansion students and staff! Good morning!

I said it loud and proud as I could with a great big smile on my face.

I want to start by saying thank you! Thank you to all of the staff, students, parents, and community members who supported Strawberry Mansion at the school reorganization meeting last night. We proved that we can come together as a community to voice our concerns en masse and demand to be heard in a peaceful manner.

We all walk through the doors of Strawberry Mansion every day. We know our school is not perfect, but there are visible signs that we are working hard to get it right. What has happened here over the years has nothing to do with you, my children. We are dealing with the effects of adults refusing to lead, serve, and use their influence to make conditions better for you. What I need for you to do is to continue to come to school. Work hard so that you can go to college and make a better life for yourself and your family. I know I have said it before, but education really can change your life. Take it from me. I sat where you sat, and lived where you lived, but now I get the chance to see life all because I decided to give that thing called education a try. Come to school, young people. You have tried many other "distractors" that promise a quick fix to a better life, and none of them have worked. But please, give education a try.

Right now, all we can do is go about our busy lives and wait on the final recommendations on school closures. We must wait to hear the final word on our football team. The last thing we have to iron out with the school district is the permit for the practice field. Once we figure that out, there will be nothing standing in the way of our first-ever football team. The athletic director and our friends from the Justice Department are working to secure that permit, so hold on and think positive about it all. You and your families made me so very proud last night. We had our say, and that is what matters. I love you, young people. Thank you for all the support. . . . And *remember*: if nobody told you they loved you today, remember I do, and I always will. Let's go everybody. Let's go.

While we waited for the verdict to come in, it was business as usual at Strawberry Mansion High School. The teachers continued to struggle with the instructional program, and the students tried desperately to hold onto their power in the school, but we were making progress every day.

Mastering small group instruction was the hardest part of the instructional program for many teachers. They were not used to managing a class and giving undivided attention to students who needed it most. As time passed, those teachers tried to avoid conducting small group instruction. But they ran up against the students of the teachers who embraced small group instruction the most. Since the students found it beneficial in their other classes, they would hold the teachers accountable for the small group instruction in all of their classes.

Small group instruction was not only making a difference in the students' academic skills, but it was also a vehicle to help build positive relationships between the teachers and the students. Teachers used small group instruction time to get to know the students as well as a time to remediate them. It was the time of day when the teachers had the chance to really know the students and their challenges.

The workload, in combination with the difficult student behavior, contributed to teacher absenteeism and resignations, but the teachers who were committed to the change handled it all in stride. They covered classes so that no student sat without a teacher.

Common planning time with the teachers was also very important. Once a week during preparation time, the teaching staff would meet to discuss teaching, learning, and the school climate. In order to improve test scores, have fun while learning, reduce serious incidents, and produce an environment for teaching and learning to thrive, emphasis had to be placed on instruction, but providing quality instruction was difficult for many of the veteran teachers. Trying to get them to introduce the lesson, model new content, provide guided practice, review guided practice, give independent practice, hold small groups during independent practice, and issue an exit ticket for assessment was too much for many of them to handle. The majority of the veteran teachers were used to just assigning graphic organizers as the entire lesson day after day. Trying to rid them of this practice was difficult. Instruction needed attention in order for the students to learn.

To get the teachers to understand the importance of delivering instruction, we displayed their students' data. We would focus only on the children who came to school every day and were never a discipline problem. We used this strategy because the teachers would always use the excuse that the students were not learning because they were not in school. We did not display the data to embarrass anyone, but we wanted to show the teachers that students who come to school every day and are well behaved should not be failing in every area. We also continuously displayed the data of the state test scores from the middle school, and we talked about how we had to make up for the gaps in student learning. After displaying the data, we often held professional development on writing effective lesson plans that addressed the state standards. Then we would walk the teachers through every part of the seven-step lesson plan we used at Rhodes. I never moved away from that instructional model because it had worked for me in two other schools, and I was certain it could work at Mansion if the teachers would commit to learning how to use it effectively. I would tell them that teaching is an art they must practice often for perfection. When teachers simply refused to accept the guidance and support and failed to adhere to the mandates they had been given, I had no problem completing the appropriate paperwork to get rid of them, and that was a known fact.

All in all, we were making academic strides as we waited. The teachers who were committed to the change worked on improving their instruction and building meaningful relationships with the students. A month after the school closure meeting, the School Reform Commission (SRC) held their final community meeting on school closures. The SRC chambers is not a large space, and many schools were up for closure, so two of the teachers and the same two community leaders and I attended the meeting. Both teachers and one community leader delivered closing remarks for why Strawberry Mansion should be reconsidered for closure in a powerful way. I felt that they should have the final voice because they had worked so hard to keep the school open. This was their reward. There was no reaction from the SRC members, but we left knowing that we had given it our best shot. All we could do now was to continue to wait. Four days later on Tuesday, February 19, 2013, at 1:42 a.m., the Facilities Master Plan AMENDED Recommendations were sent out:

> Yesterday, we finalized several changes to the Facilities Master Plan recommendations released in December. More than a dozen recommendations were modified as a result of the District's review and analysis of feedback and comments gathered during the extensive

outreach conducted from December 2012 through February 2013.

outreach conducted from December 2012 through February 2013. Approximately 5,000 people attended the District's 21 community meetings, and we received 40 community proposals from principals, students, parents, and community organizations.

The recommendation that affected your school and community was modified. The amended recommendation is below:

**Strawberry Mansion High School will remain open at its current location.**

I am grateful for the time and energy that your school community invested in voicing concerns about the Facilities Master Plan. I do believe that the amended recommendation addresses the concerns raised by parents, students, and educators like you. I am confident these changes will allow us to move forward on the path to providing better options for families.

The new recommendations call for the closure of 29 buildings, including 15 elementary schools, five middle schools, nine high schools, and one lease termination. To accomplish the 29 building closures, the District will need to change a number of grade configurations. The new recommendations will result in an overall District building utilization rate of approximately 78 percent, a projected increase of 11 percent from the current rate of 67 percent.

Thank you again for your patience and support during this process.

We had saved Strawberry Mansion High School from closure. We had demonstrated what a committed group of people with a clear focus could do when we all worked together. It felt good to win! It gave my students a real-life example of what could happen if you work hard and believe in a cause.

To ensure that Strawberry Mansion High School received the support it needed, the superintendent also announced that Strawberry Mansion High School would be part of the district's fourth cohort in the Renaissance Schools Initiatives. This cohort of schools was called Promise Academies. These were the schools that were academically low performing, with the majority of the student body living in poverty. Extra funding would come to support the school for many years. However, what came immediately was my ability to release 50 percent of the teaching and support staff at the end of the school year.

Turning over 50 percent of the staff was the biggest gift of all. To have the ability to rid the school of the teachers who gave out work packets so that the students would not come to class; teachers who only knew how to instruct by having the students make graphic organizers and copy out of the textbook; teachers who would not get out of their chairs to teach; teachers who lied to get students arrested; teachers who refused to improve their instruction; and teachers who refused to enforce the non-negotiable rules. More resources was important, but having the ability to start again with the staff would spare the students additional years of an inferior education.

In the weeks that followed the announcement that the school would stay open and our conversion to a Promise Academy, we planned a big celebration for the community. We had a lot to celebrate! We decided to have a Saturday block party. We received a permit to close the street outside the school and had a party, D.J. and all. The local business community donated food, and we had face painting, a moon bounce, and art projects for the kids. We had a lot of free giveaways for the adults, too: books, energy-saving lightbulbs, food, and local business information, to name a few. We even had a station to sign students up for local summer jobs. Members from the Philadelphia City Council, the Department of Justice, and the Philadelphia Eagles came to speak to the residents and to say job well done. It was a great event. And to cap it all off, at the "thank you" block party, it was announced that the football team was really going to happen! A school that had so many problems had won two major battles in one year: a fight to stay open, and a fight to have a football team that was nearly 50 years overdue. Two battles others would not dare to pursue. Older members from the community who had wanted a football team while they were at Mansion wept at the announcement. Mansion football! Everyone thought it was impossible, but I always had hope.

After the block party, I went to my office. I sat in my blue leadership chair and thought about how things had worked out. I reviewed it all in my head in about five minutes, starting with my decision to be a principal after 20 years in the classroom. I thought about how I became a principal after only two months as a new teacher coach, how I had been the only principal in Philadelphia involved in three school mergers, and how I had discovered that schools in North Philadelphia could become "real schools" with the right leadership that held everyone accountable for the job they were paid to do. I had taken on a job like assistant superintendent when I wanted no part of the job, but it was all preparation for this battle to be won: to save a school and prove to a community that there is power in numbers and persistence, and that unwavering faith can yield unbelievable results. Fear was still there every step of the way. But hope was no longer just something we wanted; it was something we had. I ended my time alone with God with a great big *Thank You!*

## Thinking About Your Leadership

"Thank you" goes a long way. Say "thank you" as often as you can, whenever you can, for whatever reason you can, and to whomever you can. People love to hear the words "thank you" for a job well done from their leaders. Say "thank you" publicly at celebrations. Celebrations keep people energized and focused on the goals at hand. Take the time to celebrate those who help you achieve your goals.

**Examine Attentively:** Your organization's celebrations!

**Questions for You:**
- How do you celebrate company wins?
- When was the last time you said "thank you" to everyone who made your organization a success?

# 22

# Opportunity

Good Morning! Good morning, Strawberry Mansion High School students and staff, good morning! I hope you all had a great time on Saturday at our "thank you" celebration. I know I sure did. Thank you for making that day special. Love you much!

Well, we have made it to prom night with very few incidents this month. That is a sign that we are beginning to gel together as a family. I have kept my end of the bargain with you all year. I said that we were not going to close. We are not closing. I told you that we would have a football team during the 2013–2014 season, and now we have a football team. Oh, and guess what? I forgot to tell you that the helmets arrived today, proof that the team is real. I said you were going to see outside of North Philadelphia, and you have done that on our college trips and our cultural experiences. I told you that the only way for us to survive in here together every day is to have hope, to stop living your life by the motto "I do what I want," and to accept structure and discipline in your lives. The school year is winding down, and I heard my biggest compliment in the lunchroom the other day. One of your classmates called me a "fraud" and several of you overheard that comment and said, "Oh no, no, Mrs. Wayman is not a fraud. She is real. She kept all of her promises." That comment really made my day. So thank you for that vote of confidence.

Students and staff, we have been though a lot in our short time together, but here we are, about to celebrate our first prom night together. I cannot wait to see you all dressed up in your beautiful clothes with your beautiful selves. You know I have to say it: I need you to be on your best behavior tonight. I do not want any drama at the prom. It is your night to shine and to be proud of your accomplishments. I know you are wondering whether I will be at the prom, and my answer is yes. Remember, I told you I am going to out-dress you all, so if you want to see me you must come to the prom. I think I am going to wear red! I hope to see you at the prom! Staff, please remember that you are also invited to attend the prom. I hope to see you there as well. Have a great day, and remember—if nobody told you they loved you today, remember I do and I always will. Let's go. It is learning time.

After the conclusion of my morning announcements, I sat back in my blue leadership chair, closed my eyes, and wondered how it would all turn out: not the prom, not the school year, but the "special." I sat there thinking about my decision not to announce that tonight was also the airing of the *Nightline* "Hidden America" TV special.

Three weeks into the school year in early September, while I was still trying to figure out how to lead Strawberry Mansion High School, I received a call from a school district representative. She said she was calling to inform me that the superintendent had granted ABC News access to film persistently dangerous schools here in Philadelphia. They were trying to make a decision on the featured site, so they asked for permission to visit all of the persistently dangerous schools. Shortly after the phone call, I received an email from the show's senior producer, Claire Weinraub. We arranged a time to meet, and she showed up with camera in hand. The producer told me all about the project and my rights with regard to the footage. I asked if I could get a preview of the special before it aired, and she said "No." That made me nervous. But the superintendent had given his permission to be there, and nothing was definite, so I continued to listen to the particulars. Deep inside, I knew they were not going to select Strawberry Mansion.

While engaged in the conversation with the producer and deep in my own thoughts about the project, I heard a frantic call for assistance over the walkie-talkie. "Mrs. Wayman, Mrs. Wayman come down here, come down here. I smell marijuana." The call came from a voice I did not recognize. I jumped up and headed toward my office exit. "Can I come with my camera?" the producer asked. "I don't care," I replied. "You have permission to be here, so let's go." We ran downstairs and found the cafeteria supervisor standing in a room near the cafeteria, holding the walkie-talkie and sniffing his nose in the air. "You smell that?" he asked. "That marijuana?" The producer and I stood there with the cameras rolling. I said I didn't smell anything, and asked him whether he actually saw anybody smoking marijuana. "No," he responded, "but it can be on their hands for a while after smoking." I was angry that he would waste my time this way, especially in front of the producer and on camera. "Sir," I said, "I do not know who you are, but don't you ever yell anything over my walkie-talkie that you cannot prove. Do you understand that?" I hated that many of the adults in the school and other schools like it treated the students like criminals. I even had one of my officers tell me, "They are all dangerous, don't you know that?" I said no, they are not all dangerous—and never treat them like criminals.

After that incident, the producer asked if that happened a lot, and I said that it did. We went back to my office, and she continued to tell me more about the project. It sounded very interesting, but I did not like to give interviews. When I was assistant superintendent, I never gave interviews. It was an on-going joke with the communications department. But there was something different about this project.

After the producer left, I called the district representative and asked whether I had to consent to the project. I wanted to know whether it was a directive from the superintendent. She responded by saying that other principals had declined, so I could do the same. She went on to say that if we were chosen as the featured school, it would be my decision whether to allow them to stay or not.

After I hung up from the call, I sat back in my blue leadership chair and thought about this opportunity. It could not have come at a worse time. Just three weeks into the school year I was still irritated at the school district for allowing these schools to merge together, and I was irritated with myself for thinking I could handle such a task. I did not want to do it out of my own anger. I took the time to think about it and decided that if we were the featured school it would not be a coincidence; it was something that was destined. It was time for everyone to see what my children had to endure to get an education. I wanted the world to see what would happen as a result of school mergers in very dangerous neighborhoods. I wanted the world to see the real effects of closures. I wanted the world to see the educational environment compared to those in the rest of the world, I wanted the world to realize that it was not the students' fault. I wanted the world to see what it took to educate children who lived in poverty with emotional trauma and a system that struggled to handle their needs. I wanted the world to see that if I could get the students to trust that I was there because I cared about them, it would make a difference. I felt that this opportunity must be a gift from God. God wanted the world to see what my children had to endure day after day in order to get an education. God wanted the world to see that love was the only thing that could lessen the fear. My mind was made up. I would say yes if we were asked to be the featured school.

Diane Sawyer and her team selected Strawberry Mansion to feature. During the year-long filming process, they had the chance to see a lot: the fighting, the drugs, the pain of the teachers and staff, the 94 cameras used to protect the school, the strategies used to transform the school, the school closure meeting, the sadness in the eyes of the children who were assaulted day after day, and all of the many other effects of poverty. They also saw my challenges: trying to keep the peace day after day, trying to build relationships with very challenging students, trying to create a structure for their lives to live by, trying to teach them core values, trying to convince them to stay in school and come back to school, and trying to find a way to pay for them to go to college. They saw it all. When I laughed, and when I cried. It was all just so difficult—but I was the leader, and I was determined to lead every day. My students' education depended on it.

When the year-long filming was completed and it was time for the special to air, I grew nervous because I knew what they had filmed and I was not sure how my students and I would be portrayed. I was so worried that I felt compelled to send them an email the evening before it was set to air on its original date:

Dear Producers,
I have reflected about this project over and over again. The only thing that I pray is that the world does not see my children as bad people. They are victims of their own circumstances. They are not bad children, but children who need support, education, and love.

I understand that this is television, and television likes sensationalism, but please do not care so much about the ratings that the real story gets lost. The story should evolve into a story about the responsibility of the educational system, parents, and communities to support disadvantaged youth.

Please do not make it sound so hopeless that the audience believes that my children do not deserve to be educated. I in no way want to bring any more pain or disgrace to them and the community in which they live. I agreed to support the district in their efforts to prove to the world that ALL children will rise to the expectations set before them, and that ALL children deserve to be educated in a safe, organized environment.
Thank You,
Linda Cliatt-Wayman

Immediately after I sent that email, I received a message that the show would not be aired the next day because of the deadly tornados on the opposite side of the country. The date was pushed back. Some call it a coincidence. I call it God intervening to give the producers enough time to tell the real story. So the special was rescheduled to air nationally on the same night as our prom.

During my morning announcements, I did not tell them that the *Nightline* special would air that night because I did not want them to worry about how they would be portrayed. I wanted them to just think about their prom. I wanted them to have one night free from pain and worry. I wanted their prom night to be everything they ever dreamed it would be.

The prom was held at a museum in the park not far from the school. Even though it was minutes away from the school, there were no signs of poverty inside. The venue was stunning, and so were the students. One of the first things that captured my attention and broke my heart at the same time was the sight of one of my students and her three-year-old baby. They were dressed alike. She explained that her baby was her date. I allowed them to take pictures, but asked her grandmother to take the baby home for safety reasons. She just wanted to take pictures with her baby to remember the moment. I thought about what could have motivated her to do such a thing.

I arrived at the prom dressed in red, as I had promised. I did not go into the prom immediately. I sat on a park bench by myself, praying that I had not disgraced my children and brought them any more pain. I prayed that I was right to let the world see that these students' challenges were no fault of their own. They were victims of poverty. The fighting, the weapons, the assaults, the disrespectful behavior, the hall walking, and the "persistently dangerous" labels were all cries for help. In order to see that they were cries for help, you had to get to know them—and that is the problem. The world only sees them from the outside. They see their color, their level of poverty, their disrespectful behavior, and their disruptive actions; but many are not willing to get to know their hearts—and the pain they feel every day from having to grow up in difficult conditions. If you have never been poor, it is hard to image the pain that brings. But when you have been, as I have, you know that the pain can sometimes cause you to act out . . . to keep everyone away. Because to know me is to know my pain and my problems, and I cannot let that happen.

I was still sitting there, crying on that park bench, when one of my teachers walked up and asked, "Mrs. Wayman, are you alright?" Through my tears, I told her what I was feeling. "I should have made them show me the tape," I said. "I should not have put my students through this. I should have kept the curtains drawn, and let the world stay out. Why did I let this happen?" I felt sad at the thought that people from around the world would not understand.

The teacher told me that the show was airing right then and asked whether I wanted to see it. When I said no, she walked away.

Half an hour later, she returned with a great, big smile on her face. "Mrs. Wayman," she said, "it was accurate, and it touched my heart." I asked how the kids were and she said they were being themselves, but that it was accurate and endearing. And she said that they got the storyline right. Then she said, "Mrs. Wayman, a lot of it was about you—about you, and the love that you have for our children." We both sat there and cried.

At the sound of my students calling me into the prom, I got myself together, wiped my eyes and fixed my makeup, and went inside, relieved that my children's story was told.

As we partied through the night, my teachers' cell phones never stopped ringing. There were calls of congratulations from friends and coworkers, and calls from complete strangers all asking one simple question: "What can I do to help your children?" It was all so overwhelming. We felt so much joy that night. The students looked beautiful, and for the first time in a long time, I had hope for the world.

As the calls kept coming, we discovered that people all over the world wanted to help my children. In my wildest dreams, I did not think anything like that would happen. The story started out about persistently dangerous schools and all the fear the students had to endure, and it ended up providing so much hope for the future for many of them. The day after the prom, the teachers had to help to answer the phones. They just would not stop ringing with offers of help, prayers, and understanding from ordinary people of all races and faiths, offering to help children they had never met. And not just ordinary people wanted to help—so did one special celebrity.

One day we received a visit from a very nice lady who came to the main office. She told me that a celebrity (whose name she could not reveal) wanted to help my students. "What do you need?" she asked. For a minute I could not think of anything. I was stuck on what celebrity would want to help my children. The rapper Meek Mill attended Strawberry Mansion as a child, and had visited in December to donate money for books, so it could not be him. She then asked, "If you could have anything, what would you want?" I had never been asked that question before, so it was difficult to image the possibilities. I started to think about the next school year. They would wear uniforms, because new clothing was too expensive for the families to purchase. I could use some help purchasing the uniforms. I told her that the heat was still a problem in the winter, and that the students were often very cold when the heat was not working properly. Something to keep them warm would be nice. I also said that I would like for them to have some type of music program. She took notes, and said she would be in touch. She said she was there in person to authenticate whether the story on television was real. Before leaving the office, she turned and looked at me and said, "I will let everyone know it is real."

A few weeks later it was revealed that Drake (the music superstar) wanted to donate everything I had mentioned to the woman who came to the school: uniforms, sweatshirts to keep them warm in the winter, and much to my surprise, funds and the resources for a music studio. It did not stop there. Drake wanted to meet my students. We planned for him to come to the school, but the district refused to allow it, citing safety concerns. Drake and his team were outraged. So, since he could not come to them, he decided to bring them to him. He gave every student and teacher a ticket to his Philadelphia concert. The students went crazy with excitement.

We thought that was the end of it, but there was more to come. When we arrived at the concert, Drake took all of my students into a private area to take pictures with them and to have a conversation with them about the importance of staying in school and being true to their dreams and goals. He told them not to let anyone or anything get in the way of fulfilling their dreams. He told them how he got started in the business, and he also told them some very private parts of his life in order to relate to them. He talked about his family and his school experiences. That was my favorite part of the encounter. It was so special and heartwarming that I will keep the particulars of that conversation between Drake and the Strawberry Mansion family. A star took time out of his busy day to give my students something they needed more than things: time from caring adults. When we all left the room to head to the concert, my students were smiling from ear to ear. As we walked up the stairs, an announcement came through the public address system: "The show has been cancelled and will be rescheduled." We stood there in shock. The show was canceled, but he never mentioned that while speaking with my students. They never gave the reason for cancelling the show. While thousands of fans were waiting for the concert to begin, he took the time to meet with my students, and then he cancelled his concert. It was all so overwhelming!

Everyone walked out of the concert hall outraged that the concert had been cancelled, but my students left proud that they were the only people to see him that night. Drake cared that much about my students that he wanted them to feel special. For the first time, they had a one up on everyone else. It was priceless.

The next day, Drake's very special OVO Sound team called to say that all of the students would get free tickets to the re-scheduled show. When that day arrived, we all filed into the sta-dium on time, and full of anticipation. We had the best seats in the house. When the lights came up and Drake walked onstage wearing the same Strawberry Mansion sweatshirt he had bought the students to stay warm; they went wild. He looked so relaxed and content when he walked out. He made the students so happy that day. I did not know much about Drake before this encounter, but what I know now is that he is one very special young man. By caring for children who needed help, he will always have God's blessing on his career.

I sat in my blue leadership chair the day after the prom as the phones rang off the hook, and marveled. There really are people who care, recognize, and sympathize in the world. The ABC team's work had changed many of my students' lives. I was so happy that I had not let my fear overshadow my hope that they would tell my students' real story. That evening, I went home and wrote a formal thank-you letter to the ABC team.

Dear ABC Family,
Thank you seems too simple a phrase for what the ABC Family has done for my students and the school community of Straw-berry Mansion High School. For years, my students have endured receiving an inferior education, being victims of poor living con-ditions, and coping with the oppressive forces of poverty. The toll of being exposed to these three factors, year after year, has

left many of my students bitter, angry, and sad. Violence manifests itself when you hold onto so much pain and are not able to release your emotions in a positive matter; my students often are burdened with this reality.

Then one day, your team set out to find a school that was plagued by years of being on the Persistently Dangerous Schools list. I do not know what you expected to find. I am sure you found it at Mansion, but besides seeing the violence you were also able to see that there are a lot of underlying factors that contribute to the violence. Your charge was to create a "Hidden America" special that told the Persistently Dangerous School story, but in doing that, you were able to let the world see that my students are not mean people; they are children in crisis. You were able to show America and the world that when children are in crisis, horrible things can happen. You were able to open viewers' minds and consider their past impressions of students like mine. I am so grateful that your viewers saw what I see every day: children in pain who need attention, something to live for, and people to believe in them.

With the donations we received, we have been able to provide more traditional high school experiences for our students. The kind of high school experiences children all over America experience every day: wearing uniforms, carrying book bags, taking trips, having novels to take home to read, and taking the PSAT and ACT. We were able to pay for all of these things that normally would be considered "extras" here. We are now able to buy jackets for the football team to reward them for a job well done, and warm-up suits for the basketball team because every other school has them. These seemingly small things give my students reasons to stay in school. We can now pay for our brightest students to take SAT prep in 10th and 11th grades, so that when they are in 12th grade, they can really compete to get into good colleges. In addition, there is money for student scholarships now and in the near future. When our recent graduates come to the school to tell us that they cannot return to college or trade school because they have a $1,000 balance, we are able to offer assistance so that they can attend another year. We have been able to expose our students to many colleges through trips. You have no idea how powerful it is to take my students on so many college and trade school trips. They get a chance to see what is possible. You must see them when they return; they look so happy. Just to be out of the neighborhood and see how others make it in the world, it becomes possible for them in their minds. The greatest joy for me is when my young men with troubled pasts come back from a trip and seek me out to say, "Okay, Wayman, I will give that school a try." These are the young men who the day before or the week before may have been incarcerated or on a path to prison.

The biggest thing that your series has done is to help me reinforce for my students and the community that violence in young children is a cry for help, not a way of life. ABC Family, you heard their cries, and so did many of your viewers, even Drake. Drake's donation will allow my students to share their talents with the world. How special is that?

Your special challenged viewers to move beyond the stereotypes about why children may fight. You showed the world that if they help, life can be better for these students. You created a way for my students' talents to be shared with the world. You allowed the whole community to see that Mansion is a SCHOOL, not a place to hang out and await a too-common lifetime in poverty, but a place where dreams can begin. Most of all, you helped me give my students hope for the future. That may not seem like much, but in this community, it is everything. Every time I think about the hope you helped me to reinforce, my heart and soul skip a beat. People come into your life for a season. Fortunately, your generosity will help me extend the seasons long after we are all gone from this earth. Together, we have invested in children, and my children are now more able to experience and change a world we may never see—a world will be blessed by future leaders it may otherwise never have known.

Please continue to find stories and children like mine who need your help, Hidden America. . . . WOW! Our problem was once hidden, but because of this program, the world now knows that situations like mine exist all over America. It is our charge to change the educational inequities that exist in America.

All children, no matter their background, deserve a high-quality education and the opportunity to be their best selves.

"Fear and Hope" was the title of the program; because you cared, there is no longer fear before hope. Hope now comes before fear, and for that, I am forever grateful. To God be the glory for the things you have done. A thousand thank-you's would not be enough for what you have done for my students. I just want to say thank you from the bottom of my heart.

Nelson Mandela and I see it the same way: "Hope must conquer fear. It is the only way for all of us to find the strength to go on." Thank you again, and remember that if nobody told you, ABC Family, that they loved you today, remember I do and we, the Mansion family, always will.

Sincerely,

Linda Cliatt-Wayman

Kindness and love prevailed. It demonstrated that there are many kind people in the world who are always ready to lend a helping hand. Those people are very, very special to the world.

## Thinking About Your Leadership

Sometimes in order to turn around a failing organization, you must take risks, even when others have refused. Fear will set in, but the chance of success is worth the risk and the reward will be great.

**Examine Attentively:** Your ability to seize opportunities to enhance your bottom line. Take risks!

**Questions for You:**

- Do you let fear stop you from taking risks on unconventional methods that could lead to turnaround in your organization?
- Are you a risk taker? If not, why not?

# 23

# Value

The *Nightline* team would return the following September to fulfill the second year of their contract, but for now they were gone. It was June. Time to focus on graduation and preparing for the next school year. As I sat in my blue leadership chair, I thought about my leadership team. I would often remind them that our paths did not cross by accident. We were put together in this place for a very special purpose. That statement used to puzzle them, but as time passed, they realized I was right. I needed their intellect, passion, and belief that things could change, and they needed my leadership to make a school for the students of Strawberry Mansion High School. The school now had a foundation to build upon, and that made us very proud.

While my mind continued to drift from this to that, I was also trying to decide who would receive the scholarship donations to attend college. Usually my inability to concentrate meant we were going to have a terrible day. As soon as that thought crossed my mind, I heard someone scream, "Call the ambulance, the school police officer is bleeding!" I threw open my office door and my secretary yelled, "Come quick!" I followed her out the door to the front foyer, and found my officer—the one who was always smiling and calm—stretched out on the marble floor, bleeding from his head. At first glance, I thought he was dead! I immediately fell to the floor to comfort him and to assess the extent of his injuries. "What happened to him?" I yelled, but no one had an answer. There were three young men standing on the wall with the other police officers, and one was in handcuffs. The young man in handcuffs was escorted to the security office as the bell rang and students poured into the hall. A few noticed I was on the floor, and came over to see what had happened. I asked them to move back. Then, the climate staff formed a barrier so they could not see the officer on the floor.

After the school police officer was loaded into the ambulance, I ran down to the school police office. The young man in handcuffs was sitting there calmly, head bowed. This young man never got in trouble, especially never for any violent acts. I said in a very stern voice, "Why did you do that?" He looked at me with a very sad look on his face. His eyes were red and were slightly closed. His appearance and his actions led me to believe he might be on drugs. He said, "I don't know why I did that to him. I am so sorry!" He kept saying he was sorry over and over again. He never raised his voice, and he did not speak above a whisper. "Why would you force me to send you to jail?" I asked. "Why? You know I hate to have any of you arrested.? You know better." He never said a word, but I felt I had to continue. "Why would you want to ruin your life? I have taught you to always stay focused on your life and to make the right decisions. Why couldn't you just do what the officer asked you to do? You could have killed that man, do you understand that?" "I am so sorry, Mrs. Wayman," he said. "Son, he was just doing his job. It is his job to protect us. When he gives you a directive, you just adhere to it. Do you understand that?" "Yes," he said sadly, "I was just angry and upset about something else."

I left him down there in the school police office, waiting to go to jail. I was so upset. I had an officer in the hospital and a student going to jail. The two places I tried to protect my students and staff from all year.

It was now time for lunch, and the students had heard the news. Most of their questions were about the officer. Everyone liked him, students and staff alike. He was polite and courteous to everyone. I tried to reassure all of them that he would be alright, but everyone was somber. This episode brought back so many memories. When I arrived at Mansion, the officers were the topic of conversation. The students were afraid of them and wanted nothing to do with them, and the officers wanted nothing to do with the students, either. The officers had no positive expectations for the students' behavior. They thought they were all dangerous.

From the first day, I had set a clear standard for how the police would treat the students, and how the students would treat the police. One would have to respect the position of the other. The students had to accept that the police were there to protect us all. And the police had to accept that this was a school and remember that the students they served were children, so the first line of defense would always be a conversation. It was an interaction that always had to be monitored. There was no trust on either side. Trust had to be earned with time.

Good afternoon! Good afternoon, students and staff, good afternoon.

Well, we had a very difficult day today. Bad choices left one of our school police officers hurt and in the hospital. I do not know how many times I am going to have to tell you that you must think before you act. Pause, pray, mumble if you are angry, but think before you act. If you overreact, you will make a bad situation worse. But if you stop before you react, you will see that your problem is not as big as you think, and that it can be solved. It is the end of the school year. We are not turning back the hands on the clock to live in fear, and none of you is going back to the old motto "We do what we want." We already know what happens when the majority thinks like that. You must always respect the adults who are in charge. There are rules in place to keep all of us safe. If you are having a bad day, tell someone so that we can get you the help you need before you do something you will regret. Young people, we are not the enemy. We are here because we care about you and your future. As I have told you all year, if you are going to change your life, you must think about your future.

On a different note, graduation is a week away, and I am so proud of all of you who made it. Tomorrow is rehearsal. Be safe going home, and remember—if nobody told you they loved you today, remember I do, and I always will.

After dismissal, I immediately had someone take me to the hospital to see the school officer. I arrived at the hospital very concerned. I ran into a lot of school police officials on my way up in the elevator. When I arrived on his floor, we were informed that he could not have any visitors. He was undergoing tests, and they would let me know the outcome. His family, including his fellow officers, was there, so I left the hospital shaken and worried. Worried about a terrific officer and his family, and worried about what my student had done to his own life and family.

I later found out that the officer had a severe head injury, but that it was not life-threatening. He was admitted to the hospital, but released a few days later.

When asked what happened, the officer said that the student who assaulted him came in the front door with three friends, very late for school. As he scanned his ID card into the machine it started to ring, indicating that the student had been suspended. The officer told the student that he couldn't come in because he was suspended. He reminded him of the proper protocol: that students are to ask to speak to someone if they are unclear about why they are suspended and need clarification. They must then sit at the front desk until Ms. Jackson could come and speak with them about the suspension and notify their parents. The student completely ignored the entire system and the directive to stop. He walked through the scan and down the hall with his three friends. The officer followed him down the hall and repeated that he could not enter the building on suspension and that he had been asked to stop. When the officer wouldn't stop insisting that the student leave the building, the student turned around and pulled the officer's legs from under him, causing him to lose his balance and hit his head on the marble floor.

The officer never reported back to duty at Strawberry Mansion High School, or to any other school in the district for that matter. One day he came for a visit and to bring me a card for caring for him the day he was hurt. He explained that he had no ill feeling toward the young man. He just wanted him to get the help he needed. He went on to say in a very concerned voice, "The children are just troubled and traumatized by the area in which they live. The times are just different. Young people have a lot to deal with—no jobs, crime in the neighborhood. Growing up in poverty causes stress, and the only place they have to relieve that stress is school. School is their safe haven, but programs are needed to really help them." He wished me well and said he had to leave for his family. He was a great school police officer. He would be sorely missed.

I arrived to work very early on graduation day. I wanted time to review the graduation program, work on my Principal's Message, eat breakfast, and thank God that I had completed the year. I closed my eyes for a brief moment, and the entire year flashed before me. The joy and the pain. The ups and the downs. The beginnings and the ends. I thought about the mother of the young man I had met during the summer before school opened who wanted her son to come back to school. He had completed the year in Alternative Education and was on his way toward graduation the next school year. What a hero his mother was to drag her son into a school and make him do the right thing for his life. The neighborhood school was the one place she had to turn for help. The neighborhood school that accepts all children. That doesn't pick and choose by test scores, grades, disability, or attendance. The neighborhood school where children with serious social and emotional problems are forced to go to school, separated from children with higher test scores and good behavior. The neighborhood schools have become the last place to prepare traumatized students for their rightful place in the world. In the neighborhood school, they must gain knowledge and mental toughness to take on the world around them, a world that has little tolerance for them. Tolerance, understanding, opportunity, and love are needed to help young adolescents grow into adulthood confident and mentally strong.

It was graduation day. All of the challenges we had to overcome to make this day a reality had been overwhelming. We just wanted to end the year on a positive note. We wanted no fear. We only wanted to send them on their way holding onto the hope we instilled in all of them. The majority of the graduates were accepted to college or trade schools, or decided to go into the military. To reach this goal, the counselors made sure that every student had an exit plan. That plan consisted of applying for at least three colleges, even when they were unsure whether they would attend. We had taken them on enough college trips to pique their interest. We wanted them to leave school with all the paperwork completed, just in case they changed their minds over the summer. We did not want paperwork to get in the way. Our families struggled with the college application process, so we wanted to eliminate that burden for them. Many of the students did not like this requirement, but it turned out to be useful for many. The donations that came in because of the *Nightline* segment made it possible for many students to attend college—students who hadn't expected to get the chance to go to college.

As "Pomp and Circumstance" started to play, I led the class down the aisle. It was a proud moment for me. The students did not have to graduate from high school thinking that no one cared about them. They graduated knowing that they were loved by someone. They all seemed happy, and that made me happy. They also would walk away from high school knowing that Strawberry Mansion was truly a school. A school that required the seniors to pass all state-required courses, complete a senior project, have life goals, live by core values, follow a structure, and be free from the idea that "We do what we want" if it hurts them or anyone else.

While standing on the stage looking at each of them, there were a few surprises. Students I thought would never settle down, follow the school rules, and complete the requirements actually did so, and graduation was their reward. I was so proud! However, some did not make it. The streets had a hold on them that they found too difficult to break. But because we won the fight against closure, we would be there to welcome them back when they were ready to try again. The graduating class looked beautiful as they filed into their seats, and tears began to fill my eyes. My team and I had taken them to graduation safely, and educated them to the best of our ability.

The program ran smoothly, and then it was time to speak to my students for the very last time. Yes, the audience was filled with parents, teachers, and district staff, but I had written a speech with only the students in mind. In the program it was titled "Principal's Message," but for my students it was my last announcement.

So I started it with

Good evening, good evening, Strawberry Mansion High School students and staff, good evening.

The students erupted in loud applause.

From the moment I walked through the doors of Strawberry Mansion High School as your principal, I have given you many messages to think about over the intercom system, in the lunch-room, in the classroom, in the hallways, and in my office. Some of the themes of these messages were: you will have to work hard for what you get; rules are to be followed; there are consequences for your actions; keep your hands to yourself; do not touch anything that does not belong to you; you have tried everything else, now try education; and education is the only way to a better life for you and your family. Please understand that I want you to remember all of those messages, for if you follow them, they will serve you well for all of the days of your life. However, I stand here tonight before you with a heavy heart to deliver to you my last and final message in hopes that it will carry you through all the good, and not so good, days of your lives.

Here it goes. . .

In my role as principal, I have had the opportunity to have many private and personal conversations with many of you. We have laughed together and cried together, and after hearing your stories of pain and despair, the conversations always led to you feeling defeated. You would often say that because terrible things happened to you, you were not going to come to school. You were going to quit on life, you did not care what happened to you. You were just in too much pain. You even questioned "Why dream?"

On the other hand, when good things would happen for you, you would look shocked, amazed that something good could ever happen for you. And then regress to your old bad habits, because you did not want anyone to know that life was about to look better for you. Or you would even run to me and ask me not to announce or mention your good news. I would often tell you that awful things and great things happen to everyone, some far worse than others, some more glorious than others; but it was how you dealt with the pain, the hurt, and the good news that would determine the rest of your life. The question you will always have to ask yourself now that something has happened, good or bad, now what? So what? now what? Unfortunately, yesterdays do not come with do-overs.

Here are some questions I have for you:

Will you allow the past, no matter how painful, to stop you from moving forward?

Will you allow past experiences to destroy your entire life?

OR

Will you use your past to push you forward?

Today, I want to remind you that all of what has happened to you up to this moment is in the past. They are all "So what?" experiences. Use your life experiences to propel you forward toward your greatness, to help you build yourself a better life.

That brings me to "Now what?" "Now what?" is what graduation day is all about: new beginnings, new experiences, new dreams, new possibilities, and new hope for the future. Your future. It is your time now to start a new course of action for your life, a course that you must design. What will that course of action be? You must think about it immediately.

September is coming, and high school is over. What will be your nextstep? Will you go to college like you said you would? Will you go to the military, like you said you would? Will you follow the plan that you designed for yourself, or sit at home trying to come up with an easier plan that does not require additional learning, giving yourself a million excuses for why you will not go for your dreams and do what you said you would do? NOW WHAT?

Will you let all the investments that people from around the world made in you all go to waste? Or will you honor their investments and make positive decisions about your future? NOW WHAT?

Will you let pain stop you from going for your dreams and grabbing a part of this wonderful life that is rightfully yours? Or will you just go for it? NOW WHAT?

I have come to realize that, for many of you, dreaming is difficult, but think about it: the things that have happened to you thus far have not stopped you from getting to this point. Tonight is a sign that you have decided to follow the positive side of "Now what?" Keep it positive. Now what? Follow the plan you have designed for yourself with the help of your parents, guardians, teachers, and counselors. Graduate from college like you have planned, go to the military and see the world like you have planned. Do not let any person, obstacle, or situation stop you from preparing for a better life for you and your family, for if you do, you will regret it. Stay focused on the "Now what?" Keep searching and answering that question with only positive thoughts. When you are depressed or happy about something that has happened, say it over and over again. Now what? Let those words start you thinking about your next step toward accomplishing your dream. From this point on, there will be no blaming others. It is all up to you. So what? Now what?

Class of 2013, dream big, and work hard to make your dreams a reality. Study every aspect of your dream. Have faith that your dreams can come true, and remember to help someone else when you do make it.

In closing, please know that I believe in each and every one of you. That is why I demanded only excellence from you. I expect all of you to live up to your fullest potential. I expect each of you to be a blessing to your family, your community, and your country. And I simply expect you to be happy.

If you do not remember all of what I am telling you tonight, at least remember the slogan "So what? Now what?" And that will help you to remember the message of this wonderful evening. So without further ado, let me end my final announcement the same way I have ended so many other announcements this year. . .

The students roared with screaming and tears.

Remember—if nobody told you they loved you today, remember I do, and I always will.
Congratulations, Class of 2013!

Just like the school year, we had started this month in fear, but month after month until this moment, we ended with hope. Why? Because love forces you to have hope, and that was our greatest success of all: showing students and staff that they were loved and valued.

## Thinking About Your Leadership

Love makes organizations successful. Love of the work, love for the people doing the work, and love for the purpose of the work.

**Examine Attentively:** Your love for every aspect of the organization: People, Purpose, and the Possibilities.

**Questions for You:**

- Do you love your work? Do you value the people in it?
- Is your love for the bottom line transparent in every area of your organization?

# 24

# Courage

It was time for the staff to pack up for the summer. Many packed up for good. They had made it through the year, but did not want to sign on for another. Many of them were asked to leave because their actions did not align with the vision of making Strawberry Mansion the best school it could be. We had also received word that the 2013–2014 school year was sure to be even more challenging due to the lack of state funding. Even though we were promised more resources through our new "Promise Academy" label, it turns out that the only thing we received from that label was the ability to release 50 percent of the unwanted staff and adopt a uniform policy for the teachers. No extra money came for needed programs to build on the foundation we started the previous school year, because we were not exempt from the cuts in state funding. The cuts led to the loss of many key positions. We lost one counselor, one assistant principal, eight hall monitors, two conflict resolution specialists, one climate manager, and several teaching positions. The 2013–2014 school year was looking frightening. The work was very hard with the existing resources, and to do the same work without them was unimaginable for most. For me, it was just another hurdle to overcome. Changing dynamics called for a new design based on what resources were available at the time. As the leader, I was concerned but steadfast in my mission to keep everyone safe, educate the students, and provide them with hope for the future. If it had to be done with fewer resources, it had to be done with fewer resources, but the goal was the same. I had no excuses for why Strawberry Mansion could not continue to move forward. I just had to lead the charge to figure something out.

The staff filed into Room 104 for our last staff meeting of the year. I thanked them for all of their hard work and wished those who were leaving well at their next assignments. I reminded them of the urgency of this work, and all it requires to ensure that children learn, especially children who live in poverty. I was unapologetic for all of the work that had been placed on the staff in order to make Strawberry Mansion a school. I urged them to take what they learned about teaching, learning, and relationships to their new locations.

For the staff who would be remaining at Strawberry Mansion, I talked about the difficult times ahead and thanked them for their willingness to continue the progress we had made. I outlined all of the cuts in staffing, but reminded them that we would not go backward. Students would continue to go to class, they would continue to have consequences for their actions, they would continue to need 23.5 credits to graduate, and our schoolwide discipline plan would remain consistent. We would continue to instill core values and to ask them to keep coming to school. The honors program would remain strong, the literature and math classes would stay gender-separate, teachers would continue to make teaching and learning a priority, the Alternative Education Program would continue, our football team would remain strong, and we would keep pushing hope as a way to a better life. I ended with "Have a great summer. See you in September. And simply, thank you for everything."

During the summer of 2013, while I was sitting in my blue leadership chair, we received word that we had been taken off the persistently dangerous list for the first time in five years, and that test scores had slightly increased. That was immeasurable based on the challenges of the current teaching staff. The data confirmed that the foundation had been set. Even though these were great accomplishments, we did not rejoice in this news. We felt that was for others to celebrate. We instead celebrated signs of hope: actions that demonstrated the students were on the path to success. Whenever a student would say things like, "I got it now," "I want to go to college," and "Now I know what perseverance is, because I just experienced it when I went to college on a Trailways bus." When a student was able to articulate without resorting to violence: "I walked away from a confrontation because I do not want to be suspended"; or a student could clearly explain what was needed in order to be successful: "I want to graduate, but I have no one to watch my baby—will you?"; "My teachers did not give me enough homework"; "Please do not call my mother again, I will do the right thing"; or say "I am sorry" when they hurt someone and "thank you" when someone did something for them. This is what we celebrated—changes in character and effort. We knew that for our students these outcomes would carry them throughout the rest of their lives. The labels "Proficient" or "Advanced" on a state test was, as the students would say, "for the school," but the life lessons were for them.

We further celebrated the graduation of my young women from Rhodes and a few from Fitzsimons who were forced over into Strawberry Mansion due to the merger, but who wanted their diploma covers to read Rhodes or Fitzsimons. At first I hesitated to approve this request, but to honor their wishes and to stick with tradition, I gave them both covers. And we were proud of many other specific accomplishments. We celebrated the student who wanted to be on a football team when he came from the juvenile facility but now wanted to go college, and we celebrated that the young man who was dragged in with his mother over the summer came to school every single day. We breathed a sigh of relief when the young man who had been shot on the corner lived and graduated from another high school. We celebrated our drop in suspensions as a sign that the students wanted to be in school for the right reasons, not just to seek power or bully and harass people. We celebrated a beautiful school that was clean and provided heat and lights in order for students to learn. We celebrated taking the chains off the front door and having our students, staff, parents, and visitors enter the building with dignity. We celebrated winning against all odds to keep our school open, and celebrated receiving more resources to help us. We celebrated our 50-year fight to give a neighborhood school a football team so they would not be compelled to leave their neighborhoods to find a team. We celebrated taking the chains off the lockers so that the students could use them and not sit in the classroom with their coats and all of their other belonging. We celebrated that our students did not come to school in fear. We celebrated that there was no need for me to use a bullhorn; they could now hear me loud and clear. We celebrated a leadership team that was second to none. And more than anything, in the words of President Obama, we celebrated the audacity of hope!

I am often asked, "How did you get the students to conform to your system?" I reply by saying it was easy. They were waiting for a system. They wanted someone to set expectations for their learning and their behavior. They wanted someone to ensure that the teachers would teach them and not throw them into the hall. They were waiting for someone to help the police see that they were not all criminals. They wanted someone to call their home when they were absent. They wanted someone to set consequences for their behavior. They wanted a clean school, with heat and lights. They wanted to use lockers like every kid in America. They wanted positive relationships with all adults, including the police. Deep inside, they all possessed a dream but were afraid to share it because there was no one there to listen. They were waiting for someone to love them despite their problems and actions that stemmed from living in poverty.

My team and I made this all possible by having courage and vision for children who needed it most. We did not take our leadership lightly.

My children want everything every other child wants: adults who believe in them, adults who will help them, adults who have expectations for them, and adults who love them. I know that when you look at adolescents, they seem as if they are all grown up and do not need these things, but really, they need them the most. It is the age between an adult and a child when they are most misunderstood. They need guidance in order to avoid the evils of the world. They need the people surrounding them to have the courage to understand them, the courage to talk with them, the courage to look beyond what they see at first glance, the courage to guide their character, and the courage to make others do right by them. Courage is needed by the leaders to make real change happen throughout the entire organization.

## Thinking About Your Leadership

You, the leader, must possess courage in order to lead any turna-round effort. Nothing will happen without it. Everyone who wants to keep things the same will test you on small and large scales. At times, fear will step in. Keep thinking about your bottom line. You must be steadfast and willing to do what it takes to get there. You must be prepared to state your case for going the distance with your "stamp of approval" plan. Having courage is very hard. Courage is where many leaders fall. Many times you will have to make unpopular decisions, but if they are needed to complete the mission you must make the call. Ultimately, winning or losing will be on you. You may as well lead strong. Winning takes a lot of courage.

**Examine Attentively:** Your courage to lead.

**Questions for You:**

- On a survey, will your employees say you have courage? What examples would they give to demonstrate you have courage?
- Do you have the courage to do what it takes to turn around the organization you are currently leading?

# 25

# Purpose

In early September 2013, after a long summer of preparation to begin a new school year, I was asked to speak at the Pennsylvania Conference for Women, where 10,000 women gathered each year for an annual conference. This year, the featured speakers were former Secretaries of State Hillary Clinton and Madeline Albright.

I had never been a speaker at a conference, let alone a keynote speaker, so my initial reaction was to decline the offer. Instead, I asked for time to think about it. I had every intention of declining the offer until I mentioned it to one of my teachers. She said, "How are you constantly telling the students to go for it if you won't?" After thinking about her response long and hard, I contacted the conference organizers to let them know I would accept their offer. I was told I would have only seven minutes to speak. That suited me just fine, but what was I going to say in seven minutes that mattered? I had a lot of sleepless nights trying to figure out what I was going to say to thousands of women enthusiastically waiting to see former Secretary of State Hillary Clinton, not Linda Cliatt-Wayman.

In preparation for my speech, I once again retraced my leadership journey and wondered how I had arrived at this point. I started to think about the intentionality of God, who led me from "You Go" to planning to speak in front of thousands. I asked myself what the chances were that I would leave a job I loved to lead a persistently dangerous school because I heard a voice; be the principal of three schools that would later merge; have Diane Sawyer select Strawberry Mansion for a special feature, causing an avalanche of support for the school; have Drake and Meek Mill support the school in various ways; and now, have the opportunity to speak at a large conference on the same stage as Hillary Clinton. What were the chances? Based on all of those extraordinary happenings, I knew that whatever my message would be, it would be divinely inspired.

As I stood backstage waiting to be introduced, I peeped from behind the curtain and saw thousands of women sitting there, preparing to have lunch. My first thought was to run out of the building, but I sat down in an attempt to calm myself. I pretended that I was sitting in my blue leadership chair in my office. That chair was magical. It relaxed and focused me through many difficult days. Whenever I arose from that chair, I always had the answer and the confidence to take on any challenge.

I began to relax a little as I heard the laughter of my fellow speakers practicing their speeches. That was something I was not about to do. My seven-minute speech had taken me many, many hours to write. The last thing I wanted to do was second-guess myself before going on stage. The words on the paper in front of me were the words I was supposed to say. I was absolutely sure of that.

The more relaxed I became, the more I thought about leadership and how important it is to any organization. My "If you are going to lead, lead" attitude "So what? Now what?" optimism, and my slogan of love as my bottom line for children achieving ("If nobody told you they loved you today, remember I do, and I always will") had landed me in this position. But what was this experience all about? Was this carefully choreographed leadership journey only to save the lives of my students, or was it to develop me further as a leader in a way I had not anticipated? Was there another turnaround leadership lesson hidden within this onstage experience?

Before I was called to the stage, the collection of words I used to communicate my must-haves for successful leadership occupied my mind: envision, discover, select, adapt, synthesize, rollout, unveil, implement, amplify, prepare, audacity, seek, listen, customized, strength, relentless, steadfast, realize, confidence, influence, possible, opportunity, value, courage, and purpose. Out of the thousands and thousands of words in the English dictionary, these were the words that had inspired my path to the school's transformation. Words that helped make each school a school, with hope and love prevailing. Each word gave me the direction and energy I needed to make the impossible possible. Each word represented a story that gave a window into my leadership journey. Saying each word in isolation brought a feeling over me that is difficult to explain, with each word representing a sense of power. Courage was the second-to-last word in the sequence, but the first to make all the rest happen, especially the final word, purpose. I kept saying the word "courage, courage, courage" in my head as I stood up from the warm embrace of what I imagined was my blue leadership chair. Every time I repeated the word, I could feel its power easing my questioning of my purpose for being there.

I could hear the thousands grow silent as I was about to be introduced. I could not believe a crowd that size could be so silent while eating! My heart started to pound. Silently, I started to pray. "Lord, these are your words for your people. Please give me the power to say them correctly." Then they showed a clip of the *Nightline* special. I could see it from behind the stage. It brought tears to my eyes to see my story on such a big screen. I stared at the faces of my children and told myself that it was all worth it: the hours of preparation, the setbacks, the threats, the tears, the confrontations, and departing a job I loved were all worth it to see hope in the eyes of my children. Then, as the video ended and I walked out from behind the curtain, I had found the nerve to look up to see all 10,000 women standing on their feet and giving me, Linda Cliatt-Wayman, a principal, a standing ovation. Through my fear and my many tears, I started my seven-minute speech.

I described as best I could in a few short minutes the journey you have read about in this book, from being called to go to

Strawberry Mansion, to the realization that my students couldn't learn if they were living in despair, to my resolve to restore my students' hope and give them the sense that everything was possible, to the *Nightline* special and the outpouring of help from around the world. Then I closed with these thoughts:

> In closing, when I was asked to participate in this conference I first thought it was not real. Why would anyone want ME, Linda Cliatt-Wayman, to speak in the same forum as Hillary Rodham Clinton? I am only a principal.
>
> Then, in the wee hours of the morning, my faith reminded me that God uses people like me for all of HIS purposes.
>
> So, after a lot of soul searching and a lot of praying, God revealed my true purpose for being here today, and that is to remind ALL of you women of esteemed positions that YOU hold the power, the clout, the influence, leverage, pull, voice, the dominance, and jurisdiction—the ability to act or produce an effect to make this world understand that this nation must invest in the education of ALL its children if it is going to remain the wealthiest nation on earth.
>
> It is up to you to use your power to remind everyone you know that "ALL children" includes children like mine: children born into poverty, children who are homeless, children who have been incarcerated and lost their way, children with mental illness who receive no mental health services, children with all types of special needs, and children who dare to dream.
>
> Remind everyone you know that children cannot be held accountable because they were born poor; children cannot select their parents or the communities in which they live. But let's not forget that just being a citizen of the United States of America affords them the right to be given an equal chance for a bright and productive life, and that life begins with a quality education. As John Dewey once said, "Education is not preparation for life, education is life itself."
>
> So, again, I am here to tell some and remind others that you are the game changers. Because YOU exist in the world, anything

is possible for child. Remember what possibilities are—abilities or qualities that could make someone or something better in the future. You have the power behind all possibilities.

You make the difference. So please take your role seriously.

When it is time to leave this conference, please go back to your cities and towns and reach out and touch children like mine. They are everywhere, children who have lost hope along the way. Seek them out, have conversations with them, and remind them that they will be okay, because you are out there in the world, more than eager and ready to help them on their journey.

Martin Luther King Jr., once said, "Everyone has the power for greatness—not for fame, but greatness, because greatness is determined by service."

Thank you.

As I exited the stage, I received another standing ovation. All I could do was cry. I was so full of emotion because I had given this task and the task to lead Strawberry Mansion all that I had, physically and emotionally. The response to that seven-minute speech was overwhelming. Every person in the audience understood the message. It was interpreted as a call to action to help all children around the world, but mainly the children of the United States of America. It was a divinely inspired message, just as I had predicted.

The audience's reaction answered the "Why am I here?" question. I was there to remind them about adolescent students like mine. Young adult children need love and support to make their dreams come true. Oftentimes, when they are no longer small babies and have big personalities and strong opinions, we forget that they are still children hiding behind many fears. When we take the time to know and understand them, we discover that they all want the same thing: someone to CARE about them for who and what they are. High school students need patience, love, understanding, non-judgment, structure, consequences, rewards, acceptance, and a reason to dream if there is going to be a more peaceful America. So was Strawberry Mansion High School persistently dangerous? No, it was not. It was persistently neglected.

And as Diane Sawyer so poignantly pointed out to me on her visit, crime, violence, and hopelessness stem from adolescents who are neglected and live in poverty. She called these symptoms of poverty. But today, Strawberry Mansion students have hope, and please do not underestimate the power of hope.

So to answer another question that I posed, "Was this carefully choreographed leadership journey only to save the lives of my students, or was it to develop me as a leader in a way I had not anticipated?" I have concluded that the journey was for the elevation of us all. It was to elevate my students out of despair, and to elevate me out of my narrow thinking of all I could become, professionally and personally. The journey was designed for me to see the connections from purpose to purpose, leading me closer and closer to why I was created. Look back over your leadership journey. Do you see any connections? Where are all of those connections leading you? Who would have known that all of those school announcements were preparing me to use my voice to inform wider audiences of the cries of students like mine all around this nation? I am a messenger as well as a leader, carefully positioned to remind others that ordinary people are the lifeline to the success of others in need. Therefore, "service" and "significance" rounded out my collection of words to communicate successful leadership. Today, I use my words to speak to businesses, nonprofits, and educators about the importance of using their leadership positions to serve and to influence others to advocate for adolescents in need in their communities. They need all of our expertise to guide them to see life in a positive way. And last, I remind leaders that if they really want to make their organization a success, find some way to give of themselves to a cause that needs them, and watch everything they touch become successful.

In the days that followed that speech, Strawberry Mansion had every resource it needed. Many of the women at the conference were business leaders. They took the message of power and influence to heart, and many of them gave of their time and resources. Because of their generosity, more children went to college, and over 40 new programs were added to the school. It really does take a village to raise a child in poverty. My leadership was a call-to-action, a call to serve. And because so many responded to the call to support Strawberry Mansion High School, it is no longer persistently dangerous or persistently neglected.

And now it's time to say "thank you" to **YOU** for taking this leadership journey with me. I truly hope that the words I have selected and the examples I have provided through real experiences gave you some insight into your own leadership challenges and triggered some solutions. Leadership is difficult. Leadership can be scary. Leadership can bring you joy. But the true essence of leadership is success in your mission, service to others, and the use of your influence to make good things happen for others who do not have a voice. If you stay focused on those three outcomes, your leadership will take you to new heights.

As my mind drifts back to 2003, when my leadership journey began, I can see the catalog displaying all of the desk chairs. I still wonder why I selected blue as my chair color. While waiting for school to begin the day after the speech, I decided to search Google to see what the color blue symbolized. I saw words like "creativity," "tranquility," "intelligence," "loyalty," "strength," "wisdom," "sincerity," "trust," "power," "authority," "dignity," "knowledge," "confidence," and "heaven." They are all words that could act as synonyms for my collection of leadership words. Believe it or not, I also saw phrases, such as "it likes to do things its own way," "you can rely on it to take control and do the right thing in difficult times," and "blue relates to one-to-one communication, especially communication using the voice—speaking the truth through verbal self-expression—it is the teacher, the public speaker." As I read those words, all I could do was smile. That is why God led me to select blue. Blue represents my purpose. Blue represents the type of leadership that I display from day to day. Blue represents GOD. And I want my leadership to always model HIS wishes.

# Index